AVENGER FIELD

Screenplay by
KIMBERLEY KATES, CATHERINE TAYLOR
and SANDRO MONETTI

Additional dialogue by
MURIEL NAIM and ASLIGUL ARMAGAN

SPECIAL THANKS TO: Rand Institute's Natalie W. Crawford,
military historian Jay Wertz, Dr. Bruce Lee,
Dr. Jimmy Jiang and the BAFTA Newcomers Program

ISBN 978-1-66786-047-3 (Print)
ISBN 978-1-66786-048-0 (eBook)

FOREWORD

At last, this important story can be told…

Avenger Field was the top-secret Air Force training base in Sweetwater, Texas, where American female pilots flew military aircraft in World War II.

These bold women flew the most dangerous, untested planes, fell victim to sabotage and abuse but continued to pull off miracles of skill to serve their country in its most challenging years.

Their battles in the sky and on the ground, to overcome the enemy, whether it was fascism, a hostile society, a sabotaged plane or even themselves, are something I've been trying to bring to the screen for over two decades. Especially as their feats had remained classified and unacknowledged for so long.

It all began in the year 2000 when my movie producing partner Stephen Eckelberry and his wife Karen Black were working on the tale of the "WASPS" (Women's Air Force Service Pilots) which they were developing as a starring vehicle for actress Sean Young.

Although that effort didn't get off the ground, the courage and determination of the WASPs had remained in my heart and mind ever since hearing their story. It was only in the years 2016 and 2017 when I was working on a World War II film set in China that I got the impetus to see this new project through to fruition.

I learned then how American female pilots had helped the people of China during WWII by secretly flying in crucial supplies. Instantly, I knew I had to use my producing experience and knowledge of the story to assemble a team of top writers to make the world aware of these extraordinary true-life heroines.

Included in that team were some extraordinary young women of today, members of BAFTA's globally acclaimed New Talent program for rising stars. After years of research, meetings, writing and re-writing, the results of those efforts are what you hold in your hands now.

This is the script for the first episode of Avenger Field, an action-packed TV series set over multiple seasons.

It focuses on the courageous real-life female pilots and the two women who battled with the establishment and each other to bring them into the war, celebrity flying aces and bitter rivals Jackie Cochran and Nancy Love.

Their recruits were a diverse, dynamic and eccentric group who were brought to Avenger Field in cattle trucks and had all the odds against them. The Air Force was designed for men, the flying suits were too big, the authorities didn't think they were strong or smart enough to fly planes and the locals thought they were prostitutes or spies. But they had ability and belief, a passion for flying, a love of country and were determined to prove themselves.

Welcome to Avenger Field. It's going to be bumpy ride – but a thrilling one.

KIMBERLEY KATES

MAIN CHARACTERS

Our complex and compelling characters are based on real people, all fascinating rebels who constantly clash against the system, each other, and themselves.

JACKIE COCHRAN: the fastest female pilot in the world, a self-made businesswoman with a cosmetics empire, and a firm believer that women should be ladies. This is ironic, as though Jackie is beautiful and glamorous, she's seldom considered "ladylike". Ruthless, impatient and tactless, she's loyal, intelligent and determined, with a sharp sense of humor. She's achieved amazing things, and is the first to tell you about it. Raised dirt-poor in Florida as Bessie Pittman, Jackie worked in the cotton mills instead of attending school. She didn't even own shoes till she was eight. She ran away to New York, changed her name to Jacqueline Cochran, worked her way up at a 5th Avenue hair salon, then impressed multi-millionaire CEO of RKO Pictures Floyd Odlum, who divorced his wife to marry Jackie, investing in her cosmetics company empire and aviation career. Passionately patriotic and pro-military, she's obsessed with creating and commanding a women's Air Force at a time where there isn't even an Air Force yet. When her more diplomatic rival Nancy Love starts a female flying squadron first, Jackie is livid. But with friends in high places, like Eleanor Roosevelt and Walt Disney, this isn't the end of it.

NANCY LOVE: Jackie's nemesis. On the surface, Nancy is a "well bred" Martha's Vineyard type. She grew up wealthy with impeccable manners. She understands the place of women in her time. Seemingly the anti-Jackie, she's always agreeable, polite and refined. Jackie loves racing and being first, Nancy sees competition as a waste of time - she just wants to fly the best aircraft for the joy of it, and to support her country. But all is not as it seems. Nancy had to drop out of Vassar when her family went broke in the depression, but she immediately got a job – working for an airline ran by Bob Love – with whom she fell in love. They ran the airline together, and Nancy worked as a test pilot till the war started. She's had a plan to bring women pilots into the military for years, playing a long game to gain equality through gentle compromise, incremental change and being flexible. The "feminine way." To the military brass above her, she's a "good" woman who follows the rules. Jackie is obsessed with gaining military power, but Nancy just sees a sensible solution to a simple problem and has no desire to be a leader. But she is prepared to step up to command – especially if the only alternative is Jackie Cochran.

GENERAL "HAP" ARNOLD: By the time he finds himself in command of America's air forces in WWII, Hap Arnold has already fought his share of battles. A West Point graduate, he trained in flight with the Wright Brothers and worked as a silent film stunt pilot in Hollywood before serving in World War I. Hap became one of the Army's first flight instructors but developed a phobia of flying as more and more of his friends died in crashes. A physical stated "in an emergency he's likely to lose his mind." But while his mental state is in question, his moral compass is never in doubt. When America enters WWII, it is Hap's duty to make major decisions - not least of which is the role of women in the air force - and he feels the pressure that goes with so much responsibility. He is not afraid to disobey orders or question the status quo if he thinks it is the right thing to do. Once he makes up his mind, he is loyal and steady to the end.

BETTY GUILD: Born and raised in Hawaii, Betty discovered a passion for flying at 14 and took lessons behind her parents' backs, pretending she was at the beach. A real tomboy, Betty was the catcher on an all-boys' baseball team, the only female student at her university, and works as a tour pilot surrounded by men. Betty has a tendency towards vanity – she's a fashionable blonde bombshell and knows it - and pride, she'll refuse to abandon a freefalling plane, risking her life to land it. She has a taste for fun and adventure, but often doesn't know when to stop. When her home – Pearl Harbor – is attacked, Betty is desperate to defend her country. She tries out for Nancy Love's WAFS – but when she's turned down, she becomes even more determined to fly for America and becomes one of Jackie Cochran's first WFTDs.

"REXY" REXROAT: From two worlds but with one mission. Rexy is a post grad engineering student in New Mexico when America joins the war. An Oglala Sioux Native American, she spent her summers at the Pine Ridge Reservation in South Dakota. Tenacious and daring, Rexy grew up in both the Native Reservation and middle class "white" society. Being an outsider has taught her self-knowledge and given her freedom to be herself, outside of conventional judgments. Sexually liberated far beyond the 1940s, Rexy knows the difference between being "easy" and a "free spirit" and she's not afraid to educate anyone who mistakes the two. When war breaks out Rexy tries to join the Marines but becomes a Rosie style riveter only to decide her future is in the sky. Although she has never been in an airplane, she trains to become a pilot. If she's going to risk her life, it's going to be for something worthwhile, like taking one of the most dangerous jobs at Avenger Field – towing targets to be shot at.

HAZEL LEE: Athletic, adventurous and determined, Hazel took one of the few jobs Chinese American women could get back then – a menial role as an elevator operator in a department store – to pay for flying lessons. She qualified as a flight instructor, a job that was so new, specialized and in demand that her skills transcended race and gender restrictions. Like many children of immigrants, Hazel felt a kinship to the "homeland" she'd never visited. When the Chinese army needed pilots, she left her Oregon home and enlisted – only to discover they wouldn't let women fly. Returning to the States, Hazel's dream to fly for her country comes true when the USA enters the war and Jackie Cochran recruits her. Hazel is never reckless - she's seen war and doesn't believe in wasting life, but she does believe strongly in duty and sacrifice for the lives of others. She's also hiding a big secret – she's gay – but will soon discover she's not alone.

CORNELIA FORT: Cornelia comes from old Nashville money, but she escaped to Sarah Lawrence where she studied under great teachers and discovered drinking, partying and politics. Family wealth enabled her to get her license faster than any other pilot, but from her first job as an instructor, no one had any idea of her background. A champion of equality and an ardent anti-fascist since before the war, she spoke against Hitler and was ready to fight for the things that make life worth living. It was a fight that would cost Cornelia her life. Cornelia becomes the first American attacked on home soil by a foreign invader. But while she survives that day, death is waiting. She will be the first female pilot to die on active duty in the USA.

Jackie Cochran and Avenger Field trainees

Avenger Field WASPs and training aircraft

Cornelia Fort WASP

Jackie Cochran pinning wings on WASP

Jackie Cochran

WASPs Training

Nancy Love

WASP Trainees with T-6 Texan

WASPs on runway

Women Air Force Service Pilots during WWII

Elizabeth Gardner

WASPs arriving at Avenger Field

Jacqueline "Jackie" Cochran

WASP Pilots pass in review at Avenger Field, Sweetwater, Texas.

AVENGER FIELD
"PILOT"

Created by
Kimberley Kates, Sandro Monetti
& Catherine Taylor

Complete Draft

Written by
Catherine Taylor, Kimberley Kates,
Asligal Armagan & Muriel Naim

"I promised these women their story
would some day be told...
this is some day." Author Unknown.

kimberley@bigscreenent.com
323.654.3400

1

TEASER

EXT. SOUTHERN MANSION - STABLES - DAY

SUPER: FORT MANOR - KENTUCKY - 1929

OVER BLACK: The laboring WHIRR of a 1920s light
airplane fighting its way through the wind.

CLOSE ON: CORNELIA FORT (9), a gangly brunette
with big brown eyes, watches the plane fly
overhead, open mouthed.

REVEAL: Cornelia stands bareback on a horse,
her arms spread to her sides, gracefully
mimicking the flight of the plane.

Slowly we begin to hear the world around her,
including a man's voice, the STABLE GROOM
begging her to get down.

                    STABLE GROOM (O.S.)
          Miss Cornelia! MISS CORNELIA!--

                                        CUT TO:

EXT. BERRY AIR FIELD - DAY

SUPER: BERRY AIRFIELD KENTUCKY - 1939 -
TEN YEARS LATER

A small silver high winged monoplane, with blue
fabric wings, pulls up into the sky and curves
upwards. The plane begins to invert. A man
yells almost inaudibly against the wind.

AUBREY (O.S.)
CORNELIA! NO--

INT. PLANE - COCKPIT - CONTINUOUS

Cornelia, now 19, is in the front pilot seat,
having the time of her life. Once precisely
vertical, she stalls the engine.

Behind her, her instructor AUBREY (28),
handsome with a Clark Gable mustache, screams,
but she can't hear him.

EXT. BERRY AIR FIELD - CONTINUOUS

On the ground, a small crowd of teenage boys
watch intently.

EXT. PLANE/SKY - CONTINUOUS

The plane seems to float, vertically in the air
for a second. Then it starts to spin.

EXT. BERRY AIR FIELD - CONTINUOUS

The teenage boys burst into cheers of delight.

INT. PLANE - COCKPIT - CONTINUOUS

Cornelia works the rudder pedals, her tongue
poking out in determination. Aubrey's scream
crescendos, an octave higher.

EXT. PLANE/SKY - CONTINUOUS

The plane comes out of the spin, levels out.

EXT. BERRY AIR FIELD - CONTINUOUS

The teenage boys applaud and scream.

INT. PLANE - MOMENTS LATER

The plane taxis to a stop. Cornelia removes her helmet and goggles, turns to face Aubrey, her grin disappearing as she sees his expression.

> AUBREY
> What the hell, Cornelia?

> CORNELIA
> (surprised)
> Saw you do it this morning,
> thought it looked like fun.
> And it was.

> AUBREY
> You can't do tricks like that--

> CORNELIA
> Why not? I have the same
> license as you?

> AUBREY
> You don't have the experience--

> CORNELIA
> Well. I do now.

The teen boys rush over, cheering. Cornelia
gives them a wave and jumps down. CLOSE ON her
boots landing on the tarmac.

                                        CUT TO:

INT. PLANE - COCKPIT - DAY

SUPER: JOHN ROGERS AIRPORT - OAHU - 1934

CLOSE ON: A petite blonde with bright blue eyes
behind flying goggles, BETTY GUILD (14) grins
and takes a deep breath--

                    BOB TICE (O.S.)
            Betty, are you ready?

Betty nods. Her face fixes in determination. She
pulls back--

Close Up: She pushes on the rudder pedals.
Blocks of wood are fastened to her boots so she
can reach the pedals.

INT./EXT. JOHN ROGERS AIRPORT/PLANE - CONTINUOUS

A small cream monoplane (a Kinner Fleet) -
looking like a large kite made from plywood -
takes off and levels out.

INT. PLANE - COCKPIT - CONTINUOUS

Betty lets out a shriek of delight. Behind her,
a dark handsome man with wide set blue eyes,

BOB TICE (late 30s), shouts in her ear over the roar of the wind.

                    BOB TICE
          Bring her around!

INT./EXT. JOHN ROGERS AIRPORT/PLANE - CONTINUOUS

The airplane banks to the left and smoothly turns 180 degrees, facing the runway again.

INT. PLANE - COCKPIT - CONTINUOUS

Bob looks impressed. Betty licks her lips in anticipation.

                    BOB TICE
          Clear. She's all yours' Betty!

Betty pulls the throttle back, grips the metal control stick. Her wooden blocks hit the rudder pedals.

INT./EXT. JOHN ROGERS AIRPORT/PLANE - CONTINUOUS

Betty flawlessly brings the airplane down to the runway, wheels touching down with barely a bounce. She taxis neatly.

EXT. JOHN ROGERS AIRPORT TARMAC - MOMENTS LATER

Betty hurriedly pulls off her flight suit, revealing a one piece swimsuit underneath.

                    BOB TICE
                   (paternally)
          We have a change room--

                     BETTY
          I'm so late, the bus will be
          here any second--

The men and boys working on the tarmac watch
her, some stop and stare, others glance with
feigned casualness.

Bob looks at them sternly, they all quickly
return to work.

Oblivious, Betty frantically packs her flight
suit, and pulls a beach outfit and espadrilles
over her swimsuit.

                    BOB TICE
            Bets, if your parents think
            you're sunbathing at the beach,
            won't they notice you only
            tanned your face?

                     BETTY
                (pauses, surprised)
            Oh! You're right! Should I fly
            in my swimsuit tomorrow?

                    BOB TICE
          I can't take you up tomorrow.

Betty looks crushed.

                    BOB TICE (CONT'D)
          It's a little soon, but you're
          ready to solo!

He smiles as Betty squeals. The men look over
again.

OPENING CREDITS: OVER MONTAGE OF GIRLS/WOMEN
LEARNING TO FLY-

All over the USA, women and girls learn to fly.
Some fly glossy expensive looking planes, some
fly rickety crop dusters on farms, some as young
as 13, others in their 60s.

ACT 1

EXT. PACIFIC ISLAND - SUNSET

SUPER: HICKAM FIELD OFFICERS' CLUB - 1941

Picturesque vista of the island OAHU, lit up by the sunset.

EXT. HICKAM OFFICERS' CLUB - SUNSET

Stilettoed feet hit the pavement. A taxi door SLAMS. Cornelia (now 22) emerges, elegant in a backless tailored jumpsuit, (think Katherine Hepburn), a flower in her dark hair.

A crowd of hundreds, 75% male uniformed military officers, 25% women dressed to the nines, jostle excitedly.

Cornelia swallows nervously as she surveys the raucous scene.

                    BETTY (O.S.)
          Cornelia!

Betty (now 21), red lipstick, blonde hair well styled, in a white and gold strappy Betty Grable style dress, approaches.

Betty takes Cornelia's arm and leads her towards the entrance. Many of the officers nod and smile at Betty.

                    CORNELIA
          Surely you haven't dated all of
          them, Honey?

                    BETTY
                   (laughs)
          I've dated *some* of them. You
          should try it. They're all
          stationed here, with nothing to
          do, is it so hard to go for a
          milkshake or a coffee?

                    CORNELIA
          You make it sound practically
          patriotic.

                    BETTY
          And *convenient* if you're living
          on a pilot's salary. Anyhow,
          I'm meeting Tack tonight.

As Betty and Cornelia reach the door, an officer
jumps in front to open it for them.

                    CUT TO: INT. HICKAM FIELD
                       OFFICERS' CLUB - LATER

A PARTY in full swing. Smoky air, dancers "cut
a rug".

EXT. HICKAM FIELD OFFICERS CLUB - NIGHT

A HAWAIIAN WAITER with a tray of Southern
Comfort, approaches a group of officers. Betty
and Cornelia are the only women with them.

                      10

                    HAWAIIAN WAITER
          Sir?

JIMMY McCAN (25), tall, fair, takes the
drinks, distributes them, handing Betty hers
ceremonially.

                       JIMMY
          Happy 21st. Chug-a-lug, Betty!

Betty sniffs it. Jimmy turns back to the
Hawaiian Waiter.

                    JIMMY (CONT'D)
          Put it on my account.

                    HAWAIIAN WAITER
          It's on the house, Sir. Betty
          used to pitch against my
          baseball team. She struck me
          out twice.

                       BETTY
                     (laughs)
          Then you must join us.

Betty hands him a spare drink, smiling with all
her charm.

                    HAWAIIAN WAITER
          Well gee... OK just quickly.

Cornelia whispers in the ear of ROBERT "TACK"
TACKABERRY (24) shorter but tougher looking
than Jimmy. He laughs, nods.

                          11

                    TACK
            (holding up his glass)
        To Betty who is a good girl -
        just as long as it's convenient
        for her.

The other officers and Cornelia toast loudly.

                    GROUP
        As long as it's convenient
        for her!

Betty LAUGHS, Cornelia finishes her drink first.

                    JIMMY
        Where did you learn to drink
        like that?

                    CORNELIA
        Sarah Lawrence, it was
        compulsory for matriculation.

INT. HICKAM FIELD OFFICERS' CLUB - MONTAGE

SUPERFAST CUT to music (with a growing ominous
tone)

Uniformed bands on stage playing a hot tune...

Officers cheer, dance, drink heavily...

Betty dances with different men, but mostly
Tack...

Cornelia and Jimmy at a table, in rich debate...

Cornelia dances and wins drinking contest...

EXT. HICKAM FIELD OFFICERS' CLUB - PARKING LOT
- LATER

Cornelia holds a cigarette, Jimmy lights it
for her. Betty and Tack lean against a 1940
Plymouth, Betty shakes her head.

                    BETTY
          My car, I drive.

                    TACK
          Then I'll escort you home.

                    BETTY
          And how will you get all the
          way back to the base?

                    TACK
          For you? I'll walk.

Betty opens her mouth to argue, stops, glances
at Tack shyly.

                    BETTY
          We have guest rooms. I'm sure
          my parents would prefer you not
          to risk your neck walking in
          the dark.

Tack grins. Betty blushes and turns to
Cornelia.

                    BETTY (CONT'D)
Need a ride?

                    CORNELIA
                (shakes her head)
I've got a student at sunrise.
Gonna walk down to the airport,
catch a nap there.

INT./EXT. BETTY'S CAR/DARK STREETS - NIGHT

Dreamy moonlight breaks the dark sky, lighting
the blue Plymouth as it glides through the
jungle road, the ocean gleaming behind them.

Betty is in her element, focused on driving,
her hair sparkling silver, oblivious to Tack
watching her admiringly.

INT./EXT. JOHN ROGERS AIRPORT - TARMAC - NIGHT

Jimmy and Cornelia stroll through the planes,
lit only by the moon. Behind them, the party is
audible in the background.

                    JIMMY
So... How fast DO you go?

                    CORNELIA
                (coyly)
Depends on the plane.

                    JIMMY
In which plane do you go
fastest?

Cornelia searches his face to see how suggestive he's being. He feigns innocence. She leads him towards a blue plane.

                    CORNELIA
          Well, Jimmy, the army planes
          may have more power, but I
          can go over 100 mph in this
          Interstate Cadet.

She leans back into the plane, Jimmy kisses her passionately.

INT. GUILD RESIDENCE DOWNSTAIRS HALLWAY - LATER

Betty sneaks down the hallway, stops by the guest room. She looks younger in her childish pale pink nightgown, robe and slippers. She takes a deep breath. Makes a decision. KNOCKS.

INT. GUILD RESIDENCE DOWNSTAIRS GUEST ROOM - CONTINUOUS

Tack lies on the bed, shirtless. A RAPPING at the door.

                    BETTY
          Tack?

Betty opens enters slowly. She stares at him, taking him in.

                    TACK
          Come in.

He deflates.

> JIMMY
> Geez, Cornelia, why won't you
> just be my girl?

> CORNELIA
> Jimmy, I have the best job in
> the world, and I don't intend
> to change that.

INT. GUILD RESIDENCE BETTY'S BEDROOM - EARLY
MORNING

Betty wakes abruptly with an uneasy feeling.
Silence. She puts her hand up to her aching
head, glances out the window at the rising sun,
lays back down.

INT. INTERSTATE CADET PLANE COCKPIT - EARLY
MORNING

Cornelia sleeps alone on the bench seat, the
flower crushed in her hair. An eerie feeling
persists.

EXT. JOHN ROGERS AIRPORT HANGAR/HICKAM FIELD
- SUNRISE

Establishing shot: two airports sit next to
each other - JOHN ROGERS (civilian) and HICKAM
FIELD (military). HICKAM FIELD has silver
military planes in a cluster. JOHN ROGERS has
an array of colorful aircraft in rows.

CUT TO:

INT. JOHN ROGERS AIRPORT AFS HANGAR - MORNING

Tourists, students, pilots, and other personnel excitedly mill around. It's 6am - peak time for flight-seeing.

Cornelia, fresh as a daisy in a colorful customized flight-suit labeled ANDREW'S AIR, strides with a tray of coffee. She nods as former students call out her name.

INT. JOHN ROGERS AIRPORT AFS HANGAR OFFICE - CONTINUOUS

A slightly grayer Bob Tice sorts through flight manifests. Cornelia hands Bob the black coffee. He nods a "thanks".

FRANK (20s) grins at Cornelia, and cheekily sips *her* coffee.

                    FRANK
          Blonde and short, just how I
          also like my women.

                    CORNELIA
          I've never truly appreciated
          being dark and tall till this
          moment.

Frank laughs, snorts coffee. Bob hands flight manifests to Cornelia and Frank. Cornelia

17

glances at it, casually lights a cigarette.
Offers to Frank, who accepts.

                    BOB
          Cornelia, you smoke too much.

                  CORNELIA
          More doctors smoke Camels than
          any other brand. Haven't you
          seen the posters?

A KNOCK on the door.

                ERNESTO (O.S.)
          Miss Fort?

EXT. JOHN ROGERS AIRPORT - AFS TARMAC - MORNING

A blue "INTERSTATE CADET S-4A" monoplane, with
"ANDREW'S AIR" on the side, whirs into action,
gains speed, gently rises.

The air is busy with brightly colored civilian
planes.

INT/EXT. CORNELIA'S BLUE PLANE/SKY - MORNING

Cornelia sits in the small cockpit. ERNESTO
SUOMALA (17) Mexican/Hawaiian, nervously
excited, sits beside her.

                  ERNESTO
          So, will I get to solo today?

                    CORNELIA
          One more landing, she's all
          yours.

Ernesto grins broadly.

                    ERNESTO
          Wish I could sneak you with me
          into the Army Air Force.

                    CORNELIA
          Honey, if I could enlist, I
          would be there in a heartbeat.

Cornelia stretches back in her seat, flexing her
long legs, looking down at the view.

Below them, the ocean, Mt. Diamond Head.
All breathtakingly beautiful against the clear
blue sky.

Beside Cornelia, a bright yellow Piper Club
rises up, piloted by Frank, who has his coffee
beside him. Behind him, two male passengers
(20s) in officer uniforms.

Frank mimes tipping his hat to Cornelia. She
mimes it back.

Frank winks at his passengers, then suddenly
dips his wing, goes underneath Cornelia's
plane.

                    ERNESTO
                  (bewildered)
        What's he doing?

                    CORNELIA
        Showing off for his friends.

                    ERNESTO
        Oh. Can we do something too?

Cornelia doesn't need to be asked twice. As
Frank's plane comes out underneath the left
side of Cornelia's plane, she banks left,
heading for Frank's plane like she's going to
crash into it.

At the last second, she accelerates and
straightens out. Frank falls for her fake out,
and pulls back on his control stick with both
hands, spilling his coffee everywhere.

Frank catches up with Cornelia, looking at her
in mock anger as he shakes the coffee off.
Cornelia and Ernesto laugh.

                    CORNELIA
          OK, and back to your lesson,
          Cadet.

She flies away. Frank's plane is quickly out of
her sight.

INT/EXT. FRANK'S YELLOW PLANE/SKY - CONTINUOUS

                      20

The men are still laughing in Frank's plane, when there's a CLANK followed by BANG BANG BANG. The cockpit turns red as Frank's head explodes into blood and glass.

INT/EXT. CORNELIA'S BLUE PLANE/SKY - MORNING

Cornelia is completely oblivious, the sound of gunshots covered by the noise of her plane. She glances at a silver military plane approaching from the ocean, but dismisses it.

> CORNELIA (CONT'D)
> Right, make the turn, follow
> the traffic pattern.

Ernesto starts turning. Cornelia glances back at the silver military plane. It's heading right for them. Fast.

Cornelia jerks the controls away from Ernesto, jams the throttle wide open and pulls up to avoid the approaching plane, missing it by fractions of an inch.

> CORNELIA (CONT'D)
> Grandstanding fat-head!

Cornelia looks down. The silver plane passes under them like a shark under a ship, their windows RATTLE violently.

A red circle on one wing... then a red circle on the other. Cornelia GASPS. A Japanese Zero.

                    ERNESTO
           Another pilot showing off?

                    CORNELIA
            No, it's Japanese!

Cornelia flips switches so fast it seems to
happen all at once, she pulls back on the yoke
and hurriedly descends towards John Rogers
Airport.

The Japanese Zero turns and follows her.

GUNFIRE rattles Cornelia's plane. She pushes
the nose down and banks fast, avoiding the
bullets.

Another BURST of fire, Cornelia banks the other
way, bullets whiz, dangerously close. She dives
back toward the airport.

Her plane WHINES at the sharp descent, a sound
sharp and sinister. The Japanese Zero gives
chase.

INT. FRANK'S YELLOW PIPER CUB - CONTINUOUS

The officers behind Frank frantically try to
take control of the plane, but it descends too
fast.

EXT. SKY OVER AIRPORTS - CONTINUOUS

A CIVILIAN PILOT (20s) in another yellow piper club, watches with horror as Frank's plane descends into the sea.

The Japanese Zero turns, pursues the Civilian Pilot's plane.

The Civilian Pilot accelerates out over the ocean, trying to outrun the Japanese Zero.

The Zero is too fast, the Cub takes a battery of bullets. The Cub drops, silently, out of the sky into the ocean.

The Japanese Zero dives and joins the first Japanese Zero, pursing Cornelia towards JOHN ROGERS AIRPORT.

INT. GUILD RESIDENCE BETTY'S BEDROOM
- CONTINUOUS

Betty pulls pillows over her head to drown out the GUNFIRE.

Her brothers EDWARD (14) and JOHN (16) run into room, jump on her bed, pull the pillows off.

                    BETTY
          Argh... whose bright idea is
          it to have drills on a Sunday
          morning?

                    EDWARD
          BETS! IT'S NOT A DRILL, WE'RE
          UNDER ATTACK!

She looks out of the window at the harbor, black smoke.

                    BETTY
                (jumping up)
          TACK! Did Tack leave???

Her brothers don't know what she's talking about.

                BETTY (CONT'D)
          He's a Naval Officer! Have you
          seen a Naval Officer in the
          house?

They shake their heads, confused. She runs out the room.

INT. GUILD RESIDENCE HALLWAY/STAIRS - MORNING

BETTY clambers to the hallway and down the stairs, yelling.

                    BETTY
          TTTTTAAAAACCCCCKKKKK!!!!!

INT. GUILD RESIDENCE HALLWAY - CONTINUOUS

Betty bolts down the corridor, opens the guest room door.

INT. GUILD RESIDENCE GUEST BEDROOM - NIGHT

The room is empty. The bed is perfectly made, military style.

                          BETTY
                    (voice cracking)
          NO!

INT/EXT. CORNELIA'S BLUE PLANE/JOHN ROGERS
AIRPORT - MORNING

Cornelia's plane dives, the Japanese Zeros fire
on her tail. Cornelia weaves and dodges to
create an unpredictable target. Bullets tear
open planes around her, but she keeps control.

Between her legs, bullets shatter the bottom of
the plane, as the Zeros try to shoot her fuel
tank.

The tarmac approaches fast, still busy with
planes and crew. Cornelia pulls back suddenly,
flattening out the descent.

                        CORNELIA
          HELL, WHERE CAN I LAND???

Bob runs onto the tarmac with signals. He waves
at Cornelia and points her to an open hangar.

She's going fast, breaks hard, bounces as she
lands. The Zeros behind her keep shooting. They
change their target.

Bob is struck down in a hail of bullets.

Cornelia GASPS as she goes past him, her brakes
SCREAM - The Japanese Zeros pull up *just* before

                           25

they hit the ground. Cornelia and Ernesto jump
from the plane. Ernesto throws up.

                    CORNELIA (CONT'D)
          BOB!!! BOB!!!

Cornelia runs to Bob, drops to her knees.

INT. GUILD RESIDENCE DRAWING ROOM - MORNING

Betty bursts in. Her parents frozen in horror
in front of a large window. The RADIO is on.
The announcer's voice wobbles.

                    RADIO
          The enemy is attacking us--

Tack emerges from the kitchen, his uniform
hastily thrown on.

                    TACK
          Can't get the operator, I--

Betty embraces him.

                    TACK (CONT'D)
          I can't get a hold of anyone.
          Where are your car keys--

                    BETTY
          Hallway, but--

Tack bolts out of the room. Betty dashes after
him.

EXT. JOHN ROGERS AIRPORT - MORNING

Cornelia frantically tries to help Bob, who
bleeds from several different wounds, one a
clearly fatal head wound.

A huge shadow passes overhead. The Zeros are
back.

Cornelia looks at Bob one last time, then
sprints for the hangar as bullets rain down.
Bullets spray Bob once more.

INT./EXT. BETTY'S CAR/ISLAND STREETS - MORNING

Betty, still in her nightgown, floors the car.
Tack finishes buttoning his uniform. The SIRENS
and BOOMS are deafening.

                    TACK
          FASTER BETTY!

                    BETTY
          This is as fast as she goes!

Behind them, a Japanese Zero flies low over the
horizon.

They focus on the road ahead, the Harbor in
front. Trying to figure out what is happening.
Zeros cluster above the Harbor.

PUTTA PUTTA PUTTA PUTTA - tarmac and road
gravel fly in the air, in a cloud of dust. Betty
SCREAMS. Tack looks up.

A Japanese Zero fires on them from above.

But the Zero is going so much faster than the car, it overtakes and can no longer fire in their direction.

The ZERO PILOT looks back. Tack makes eye contact. The pilot grins, and is gone.

More gun fire, behind them. Tack looks back, 10 more Zeroes.

                    TACK
          SORRY BETTY!

He jerks the wheel, they SCREAM and CRASH into thick jungle.

INT. JOHN ROGERS AIRPORT AFS HANGAR - MORNING

Cornelia sprints through the hangar to the noisy office.

INT. JOHN ROGERS AIRPORT AFS HANGAR OFFICE - MORNING

Cornelia throws the office door open.

                  CORNELIA
          THEY SHOT BOB! WE'RE UNDER
          ATTACK!

She looks around the office expectantly.
The window shade is still down. They're all oblivious to the dangers outside.

                    PILOT 1
                 (disbelieving)
          What are you talking about--

A MECHANIC runs into the office.

                  MECHANIC 1
                (out of breath)
          Oh my God...it's Bob...that
          plane just shot down Bob Tice!

Cornelia sinks to the floor.

BOOM. Antiaircraft guns. The ground shakes.
Disbelief melts into fear. Secretaries and
crewmen dive under desks.

The window blind opens, we push in on the view--

A vista of encroaching black smoke slowly
clears to reveal a sign: **PEARL HARBOR**. BOOM!

A nightmare vision of Armageddon plays out.
The SINISTER WHINE of descending planes becomes
deafening.

In the sky, hundreds of silver planes, diving,
firing.

A black object drops from a plane, the plane
jerks up at the release. The bomb falls...

INT. BATTLESHIP OFFICER'S CABIN PORT SIDE
- CONTINUOUS

DIN OF CREEPING GUNFIRE. Jimmy sleeps on his bunk, the ghost of a smile on his face. His pillow is stamped U.S.S. ARIZONA.

BOOM. The ship shakes. Jimmy scrambles up, desperately looks around. Out of the porthole; dense black smoke.

                    JIMMY
          TACK?

He checks the top bunk. Betty's photo taped to the frame, a label: OFF. ROBERT TACKABERRY. Bed clearly not slept in.

                    JIMMY (CONT'D)
          You lucky devil.

A moment of relief, then he freezes. Through the GUNFIRE the unmistakable WHINE of a falling bomb grows louder and louder.

Jimmy takes a deep breath, closes his eyes--

The shadow of the looming torpedo bomber blocks all light, the room goes dark. All SOUND cuts out.

EXT. PEARL HARBOR VISTA - CONTINUOUS

The bomb hits the USS ARIZONA, splintering explosions. Huge PLUMES of flame and smoke. The ship seems to disappear.

EXT. JUNGLE/ROAD/CRASHED PLYMOUTH - MORNING

Betty and Tack hold pieces of foliage over their heads as they watch the Harbor. Tack forgets the danger of the Zeroes, drops his foliage, screams in rage. Betty sinks to her knees.

EXT. JOHN ROGERS AIRPORT HANGAR/HICKAM FIELD - LATER

HICKAM FIELD is an inferno. Of the eight ships in PEARL HARBOR five are on fire, the other three sunk. The sky is full of shining silver planes, reflecting the harsh sun.

END OF ACT 1

ACT 2

INT. WASHINGTON DC. - NBC NEWS SOUNDPROOF BOOTH
- DAY

A worried Eleanor Roosevelt speaks into an NBC
microphone.

> ELEANOR ROOSEVELT
> *A word to the women in the*
> *country tonight.*

INT. JOHN ROGERS AIRPORT AFS HANGAR OFFICE
- AFTERNOON

Cornelia emerges from under the desk. The other
pilots and ground staff emerge too, checking
that it's safe now.

> ELEANOR ROOSEVELT (V.O.)
> *You cannot escape a clutch of*
> *fear at your heart--*

INT. HOSPITAL - DORM - DAY

A male DOCTOR (30s), pauses to listen to
Eleanor on the radio. A female NURSE (20s)
nudges him to pay attention to their patient,
an officer from the club the night before.

> ELEANOR ROOSEVELT (V.O.)
> *- and yet I hope that the*
> *certainty of what we have to*
> *meet...*

In agony, the Patient bites on a wedge of
wood. The nurses cut burned skin off him with
scissors, piling it beside him.

EXT. FORD ISLAND SHORELINE - DUSK

The orange sunset bleeds into the red water. An
exhausted, mainly female rescue crew search for
bodies along the shore.

Betty searches the waist high water. A wave
ripples, she sees an eyeless face below her
reflection. She HOLLERS for help.

She reaches into the water, grabs the back of
the corpse's head, but the burned skin slides
off in her hand. Betty scrambles to see the
face. It's the Hawaiian Waiter from the night
before. Her legs buckle and she retches.

A wave hits, knocking the body and Betty apart.

Desperately, Betty lunges for and grabs the
torso. She looks up defiantly, and takes a
breath, determined to overcome.

                    ELEANOR ROOSEVELT (V.O.)
          ... *will make you rise above*
          these fears.

                                        CUT TO:

INT. HICKAM FIELD OFFICERS' CLUB - AFTERNOON

Orange glow of shuttered light through hastily boarded windows. The doorway is completely shot out. A single waiter.

CORNELIA and BETTY drink cold coffee. There's a simmering rage in both of them that they suppress.

> BETTY
> The base, the harbor, the town,
> so many gone. Everything's
> changed. It won't ever be
> the same.

> CORNELIA
> No. No, it won't.

Cornelia hesitates. Reaches out to touch Betty's hand.

> CORNELIA (CONT'D)
> Betty, I'm leaving as soon as I
> can get off this island.

Betty inhales sharply.

> BETTY
> But, where're you going?
> What're you going to do?

> CORNELIA
> Not sure. But I can't stay
> here. All civilian flights are
> grounded, and I can't type or
> file. I can only fly. I'm useless.

Betty thinks it over, resigns herself, exhales slowly.

                    CORNELIA (CONT'D)
          Come with me?

                    BETTY
          They need me to stay.

                    CORNELIA
          Do they? Whatever for?

Betty is unsure. Cornelia stands, looks around the club.

                    CORNELIA (CONT'D)
          We had some good times here.

INT/EXT. BLACK AND WHITE NEWSREEL MONTAGE
(REAL FOOTAGE)

Jumpy 16mm film, with a slightly patronizing male voice over:

Cornelia steps off a ship, to a hero's welcome.

                    NEWSREADER (V.O.)
          Fresh from her miraculous
          escape at Pearl Harbor--

Cornelia gets off a train, waves to the gathered crowd.

                    NEWSREADER (V.O.)(CONT'D)
                Famous aviatrix Cornelia Fort is
                traveling selling war bonds--

Cornelia on stage, speaking passionately (and
silently.)

                    NEWSREADER (V.O.)(CONT'D)
                Because this gal won't let the
                Japs win! She's applied to the
                Army Air Forces - I wouldn't
                want to be the one to tell her
                they don't take women!

INTERVIEWER (50s) thrusts a microphone at
Cornelia. She smiles to camera, but her voice
has a vicious intensity--

                    CORNELIA
                I wish I were a man - just for
                the duration. I'd give anything
                to train to be a fighter pilot
                and then meet up with that Jap
                again.

                                        CUT TO:

INT. HICKAM FIELD AIR FORCE AIRPORT - TYPING
POOL - DAY

Betty, dressed smartly in a skirt suit, blends
into a room of similarly attired women.

Bored, she plays with wedding and engagement
rings on her finger.

She sighs and tries to re-focuses on her typewriter. She very slowly hits the keys with two fingers.

An austere looking GENERAL AUGUSTUS HARLOW (50s), exits a side office, holding a piece of paper, and heads for Betty.

                    GENERAL HARLOW
          Mrs. Tackaberry?

It takes Betty a second to realize she's Mrs. Tackaberry now.

                    BETTY
          Yes, General?

                    GENERAL HARLOW
          Are you aware there's an "O" in
          the word "count"?

Betty blushes.

                    GENERAL HARLOW (CONT'D)
          I don't understand how you're
          the only girl who's been to
          college, and easily the worst
          typist.

                    BETTY
          I didn't take typing, General,
          I was in the Civilian Pilot
          Training, and I--

But he's already gone. She balls the paper and throws it across the room into a trash-can. She makes the shot. No one notices. She sighs, then looks out the window.

EXT. HICKAM FIELD AIR FORCE AIRPORT - TARMAC
- CONTINUOUS

Ernesto with other boys in uniform looking lost as a SERGEANT (22) yells at them, pointing at a crushed fighter plane.

The Sergeant turns and sees Betty. He gives a surreptitious wave, then rolls his eyes at the incompetent boys.

INT. HICKAM FIELD AIR FORCE AIRPORT - OFFICE
- CONTINUOUS

Betty waves, ruefully. TYPIST (25), next to her, looks over.

                    TYPIST
          Is that your husband?

                    BETTY
          No no, just a friend. We were
          in the Civilian Pilot Training
          at University of Hawaii
          together.

                    TYPIST
          You're a pilot?

Betty nods. The Typist looks from the boys back
to Betty.

> TYPIST (CONT'D)
> You're much safer with us.
> Flying's just too dangerous for
> girls.

Betty glares at her typewriter as she attempts
again to type.

> CUT TO:

INT. AIRPORT - OFFICE - NIGHT

SUPER: MONTREAL - ATLANTIC FERRY ORGANIZATION -
A MONTH LATER

GENERAL HENRY "HAP" ARNOLD (53), USAAF uniform,
balding snowy white hair, dark eyebrows and
a face that always looks like he's smiling -
"Hap" is short for Happy - paces the office.

His secretary, HEATHER (22), quirky, enters,
looking nervous.

> HAP
> Well?

> HEATHER
> It's true, General Arnold.
> It's been leaked to the press.
> Hearst.

                              HAP
          Goddamn it.

Hap puts his hand to his chest suddenly, and
groans, like he's having a heart attack.

He sits at the desk, puts his head between his
knees, pulls a well worn paper bag from his
pocket and breathes deeply into it. Heather is
used to this. She ignores it.

                      HAP (CONT'D)
                    (between breaths)
          She has to leave right now.

                          HEATHER
          Or the Germans will shoot her
          out of the sky.

Hap breaks into a naughty smile as his
breathing settles.

                    HEATHER (CONT'D)
          And that would be a BAD thing,
          Sir.

                            HAP
          There's probably a downside I'm
          not seeing. Tell her to get on
          with it. When's our Washington
          flight?

                          HEATHER
          An hour... There's one other
          thing.

                    HAP
          What is it, Heather?

Heather hands him his overcoat.

                  HEATHER
          Some pilots are outside who
          wish to speak with you. And,
          er, Sir, have you ever been to
          a lynching?

EXT. AIRPORT - TARMAC - NIGHT

Ice and snow cover the fields around the tarmac.
25 male pilots stand around a makeshift podium
murmuring angrily.

Hap stands at the podium, fields questions with
misty breath.

                  PILOT 1
          She's taking bread out of our
          families' mouths!

                    HAP
          It's one flight, and she's not
          being PAID for it.

He points to the next shivering red faced
pilot.

PILOT 2

Sir, she may be a crack pilot
in her little Lady plane, but
dames got no business flying
bombers! They don't got the
strength. It's a waste of fuel
and a good plane.

HAP

She passed all the tests but
she's not taking off and
landing - Captain Carlisle
will. She's been practicing five
times a day--

PILOT 3

She's making a joke of us. How
are we supposed to face our
families with some dames taking
our jobs?

HAP

Men. I landed, two hours ago
from London, and I'm leaving
in 30 minutes for Washington. I
have the entire damn Army Air
Force to run and no time for
you whining like little girls
because you don't get to fly
the bomber. This war is just
beginning for us. You'll all
get your chance.

Hap leaves the podium, taking a steaming coffee from Heather.

                    HAP (CONT'D)
                (mutters to Heather)
          That oughta hold 'em for a bit.

He heads over to a chunky camouflage painted
LOCKHEED HUDSON V BOMBER. In the shadows
hugging the plane lurks a figure.

                    JACKIE (O.S.)
          (affected Katherine Hepburn accent)
            But I'm not *some dame*, I'm
            Jackie Cochran.

Hap jumps. The figure steps out of the shadows.

Cream skin, big brown eyes, red lips. Curled
golden hair, on a different woman would look
angelic. She's a stunner, but her eyes pierce
right through you. JACKIE COCHRAN (35),
dressed in a flight suit, fur coat and matching
earmuffs.

                    HAP
          Jesus Jackie. Don't let the men
          see you.

                    JACKIE
          Hap, they should all be fighting
          in Europe, not worrying about me.

43

                    HAP
I'm not so sure that every
pilot wants to go into combat.

                   JACKIE
Of course they do. Every true
American does. Hell, I'd give
my fortune to fly combat for the
USA.

                    HAP
                 (chuckles)
I stand corrected.

Jackie senses she's being patronized, goes on
the attack.

                   JACKIE
That's why we need women pilots
in the Air Force, Hap. We need
to take over the non combat
duties, get all our men to the
front.

This is not the first time Hap has heard this.
He sighs.

                    HAP
With what planes? We have so few.

                   JACKIE
You have 1100 now but in a
year you'll have 60,000, then
125,000.

                    HAP
                (surprised)
          That's classified.
                (dryly)
          I see your friendship with
          Eleanor Roosevelt is paying
          off. If her husband approved my
          air plans sooner, we'd have all
          the planes we need now.

                   JACKIE
          How do you think your plans
          came to be approved at all?

Hap pauses. Could this be true?

                JACKIE (CONT'D)
          Hap, this war will be won in
          the skies--

                    HAP
          That's from MY speech--

                   JACKIE
          I know, it was a good speech.

She grins at him, putting on all the charm.

                    HAP
          Women aren't strong enough to
          fly bombers--

                    JACKIE
I tell you Hap, there are few
women less athletic than I, and
I can fly a bomber--

                    HAP
You're not taking off or
landing--

                    JACKIE
I CAN take off and land. My
hand is just sore from doing it
five times a day for weeks. I
can still do it--

                    HAP
NO. Captain Carlisle will--

                    JACKIE
HAP. We WILL have more planes
than pilots and we'll need more
of both. *My* unit will free men
from picking up and delivering
planes so they can fight.
They'll be thanking us.

                    HAP
And you would head this women's
unit?

                         JACKIE
          Of course. (beat) Sooner or
          later we *will* need this, and I
          need you to promise me, when it
          happens, I will be in charge to
          do it right.

Hap thinks it over. Eventually--

                         HAP
          If--

                         JACKIE
          When—

                         HAP
          --it happens, I promise you
          will be in charge.

Jackie reaches out her right hand to shake. Hap
looks at it. It's red, and raw in places. Looks
painful. He takes it gently. She gives a firm,
hard, powerful handshake.

                                        CUT TO:

EXT. BOMBER PLANE/SKY - EARLY MORNING

The chunky camouflage HUDSON Bomber glides, mid-
flight, through the pre-dawn sky. Suddenly, all
the lights go out.

INT. BOMBER PLANE - COCKPIT - CONTINUOUS

Alarms BLEAT urgently. Smoke gently wafts into the cockpit. In the pilot seat, Jackie remains seated calmly.

CAPTAIN CARLISLE (38) dark hair, lanky, Clark Gable mustache and ears, strong Welsh accent, appears with a flashlight.

                    CARLISLE
          Fuse blow?

                    JACKIE
          Yes, but I can't tell where.

Carlisle quickly throws opens the toolbox. It's almost empty.

                    CARLISLE
          What the heck? This was full!
          Who would do this?

                    JACKIE
          The lads on base.
          Disappearances keep happening.
          I brought my own--

Jackie reaches into a large black purse with "JACKIE COCHRAN COSMETICS" written in gold, gives a wrench to Carlisle.

The plane yaws left, Jackie deftly deflects the rudder right.

                    JACKIE (CONT'D)
          I'm losing the port engine!

The plane lurches to the left again. Jackie
frantically examines the instruments to see
what's happening. No clues.

Carlisle runs to the window to look at the port
engine. Open flames reflect in his eyes.

CARLISLE PORT ENGINE ON FIRE!!

EXT. BOMBER PLANE/SKY - PORT ENGINE
- CONTINUOUS

CLOSE ON: Flames lick the smoky port engine--

INT. BOMBER PLANE - COCKPIT - CONTINUOUS

Jackie swallows and makes the sign of the
cross. (When stressed, like now, she reverts to
her real Southern accent.)

                    CARLISLE
          Emergency landing?

                    JACKIE
          Abort the mission? No chance.

Jackie pulls back the yoke with all her weight.

The nose shoots up, they ascend sharply.
Carlisle jolts, then looks down through the
hatch. Below them, green fields.

                    CARLISLE
     Jackie we're almost there! We
     bail, the plane'll crash in a
     field and--

                    JACKIE
     NO! We're SO CLOSE and if I
     deliver her with even a dent,
     it'll be centuries before
     another woman gets to fly a
     bomber.

                    CARLISLE
     You're the first woman to fly a
     bomber across the Atlantic,
     isn't that enough?

                    JACKIE
          NO.

She keeps pulling on the yoke. The plane's
ascent slows - on one engine, there's a lot
less power.

Carlisle groans as he realizes what she's
doing. He grabs oxygen masks, fits Jackie's on
her, then his.

                    CARLISLE (CONT'D)
     Keep perfectly level or she'll
     go into a tail spin and *we'll*
     end up cremated all over those
     fields!

                    JACKIE
         I KNOW!

The plane rattles, the ascent gets slower and
slower.

                    CARLISLE
         We're at 24,000 feet, the
         pistol engines can't take it--

EXT. BOMBER PLANE/SKY - PORT WING - CONTINUOUS

Close on: flames on the engine flicker as they
get less oxygen. The plane splutters and shakes
as she forces it up.

INT. BOMBER PLANE - COCKPIT - CONTINUOUS

The altimeter climbs - 24,100, 24,500,
24,700...

Carlisle braces himself. Jackie turns off the
port engine.

                    JACKIE
         Shutting down port engine...
         NOW!!

EXT. BOMBER PLANE/SKY - PORT WING - CONTINUOUS

Close on: The port engine whirs and stops.

INT. BOMBER PLANE - COCKPIT - CONTINUOUS

She rams the yoke forwards. The plane jerks
then dives hard.

EXT. BOMBER PLANE/SKY - PORT WING - CONTINUOUS

Close on: The flames disappear, leaving a
smoking engine.

INT. BOMBER PLANE - COCKPIT - CONTINUOUS

Carlisle covers his ears in pain as they pop.

Jackie slowly releases the yoke. Carlisle
checks the engine.

EXT. BOMBER PLANE/SKY - PORT ENGINE - CONTINUOUS

Carlisle's point of view: The fire is gone.

INT. BOMBER PLANE - COCKPIT - CONTINUOUS

                    JACKIE (CONT'D)
          It's out, right?

                    CARLISLE
          It's out. *You've* flipped your
          lid. Can you restart the
          engine?

Jackie restarts the port engine. It splutters
and dies. The fuel gauge for the port engine
is empty. She looks at the other fuel gauge.
Almost empty.

She pulls the yoke up gently to lessen the angle of descent, and decreases her speed. The plane splutters.

                    JACKIE
          We're out of fuel.

Carlisle looks at her to see if she's serious. She nods.

                    CARLISLE
          Shit. Jack, you're the Queen of
          crash landings--

                    JACKIE
          I NEVER crash. Incidental
          landings, yes, I've had over
          100--

                    CARLISLE
          CAN YOU MAKE IT?

Jackie thinks for a quick second. Calculates.

                    JACKIE
          Yes, but I'm not allowed to
          land?

They exchange a look. Both nod. Carlisle picks up the radio, mutters into it urgently. The plane splutters again.

                    JACKIE (CONT'D)
          There's the base!

Jackie's point of view: Prestwick Air Base ahead below. Jackie adjusts her course, turns off the mags and selector. She cuts the engine, their NOISE drops away.

The plane stops spluttering, smoothes into a full glide.

Jackie pulls back the yoke, forces the plane into the highest angle of descent possible, pulling so hard she's shaking.

Carlisle grabs onto her and pulls back with all his force. The only sound: the plane's RATTLE and Jackie's heavy BREATH.

EXT. PRESTWICK AIR BASE - RUNWAY - CONTINUOUS

Worried ground crew see the plane above approaching too fast and too low. They scatter from the runway.

INT. BOMBER PLANE - COCKPIT - CONTINUOUS

Jackie pulls back on the yoke with all her strength. As soon as they clear the buildings at the airport, she drops the landing gear. They hit the runway with a CLANK.

Jackie's right hand on the hand brake is bright red, raw and shaking, but she holds tight as they slow.

The plane stops. Carlisle takes Jackie's seat fast.

Jackie gets a "perk up stick"- black tube of cosmetics - from her make up case. She fixes her hair, lipstick and powder.

Jackie covers her red raw hand with foundation, blends until there is no trace of injury or weakness. Admires her work.

                                        CUT TO:

INT/EXT. BLACK AND WHITE NEWSREEL MONTAGE (REAL FOOTAGE):

Time lapse: Aerial shots of fields becoming airports. Chrysler and GM factories end manufacture of cars. Aircrafts come out of the factories instead.

                NEWSREADER (V.O.)
           Air power is the way! Chrysler
           and GM have swapped making cars
           for airplanes- Bombers to be
           precise.

"ROSIE THE RIVETERS" - women in navy overalls and red bandanas- work side by side in the aircraft factories.

                NEWSREADER (V.O.)
           With women working 24 hours a
           day, one B24 Liberator Bomber
           comes off the factory line
           every 63 minutes.

INT. B24 AIRCRAFT FACTORY - WORK STATION - DAY

The same scene: women of all shapes, sizes, and
ethnicities, all in blue coveralls. A whole
factory of "Rosies," riveting. Above them,
cranes move plane parts throughout the factory.

OLA "REXY" REXROAT (24) olive skin, green
eyes, dark hair in a red bandana, hangs upside
down from a platform, red-faced and enjoying
swinging a little as she rivets along a seam on
the upper fuselage of a B24 cockpit.

MAE (30s, African American), strong-looking
and cheerful, rivets the same cockpit, but from
inside.

> MAE
> -- I told him: if you want
> Mama to teach you piano again,
> you gonna have to learn by
> candlelight.

> REXY
> How'd he take it?

> MAE
> He went looking for candles.
> Not usually allowed to play
> with matches, so he's over the
> moon.

> REXY
> A man after my own heart. I was
> always getting in trouble as a
> kid for playing with fire.

                    MAE
         He's 6, but if you're want a
         man--

                    REXY
         Not a chance. I--

A CRUNCHING CRASH. Something metallic falls
from a crane so fast it's almost invisible.

SLOW MOTION: Rexy's face is splashed with
blood. Below her, so is Mae's. They look at
each other, ashen, then look down. There's a
blood covered hand on the floor of the cockpit.

They both SCREAM. END SLOW MOTION.

                 END OF ACT 2

ACT 3

INT. B24 AIRCRAFT FACTORY - WORK STATION
- CONTINUOUS

Rexy lifts her arms up. One hand... then
another. Mae's right hand is severed. BLOOD
spurts everywhere. Rexy makes eye contact with
a woman in the crowd that's starting to form.

                    REXY
          CALL AN AMBULANCE!

The woman nods, and disappears. Rexy takes the
bandana off her hair and wraps it around Mae's
wrist as a tourniquet.

                    MAE
               (hysterically)
          My hand. My hand.

                  WOMAN 1
          What happened?

Rexy ties off the tourniquet, holds the hand
above Mae's head. The blood flow slows. Rexy
jumps down to the floor, looks Mae in the eye
and speaks soothingly.

                    REXY
          Mae. It looks bad, it hurts,
          but it's going to be OK.
          Think about childbirth, you
          got through that. You'll get
          through this.

Mae snorts weakly. Nods. The foreman, NED (40s)
runs over.

> NED
> Ambulance is on its way, told
> it to come to the front.

Convulsing with pain, Mae bears down and
breathes to stand up. Rexy puts Mae's arm over
her shoulder, other workers gather to help
carry Mae. They exit slowly.

Ned addresses the crowd.

> NED (CONT'D)
> Take a few minutes if you need
> it. When you're ready, go back
> to work. (off their scared
> faces) It's the only thing we
> can do.

The crowd dissipates. Rexy and Mae leave a
trail of blood.

CUT TO:

INT. B24 AIRCRAFT FACTORY - WORK STATION
- AFTERNOON

Rexy scrubs Mae's blood from the cockpit. She
stops, looks around. Tears in her eyes. She
bites her lip. It bleeds but the tears stop.

INT. B24 AIRCRAFT FACTORY - CLOCKING OFF TIME

The women leave somberly. Rexy, uniform still covered in dried blood, hands Ned an envelope.

                    REXY
          I'm so sorry, Ned.

                    NED
          We need you Rexy. You're a
          great worker. Take a few
          days...

                    REXY
          I can't. What we do is
          important, but if I'm risking my
          life, it's gotta be worth it.

                                        CUT TO:

INT. SOUTHERN MANSION - CORNELIA'S BEDROOM
- DAY

Cornelia looks into a full length mirror.
Behind her the room looks elegant and
expensive. By contrast, Cornelia is wearing
a poofy pink dress. She looks ridiculous. She
knows it.

                    CORNELIA
          No, Mother. No one wants to buy
          war bonds from Glinda, the Good
          Witch.

An elegant silver haired woman who resembles
a smaller version of Cornelia, MRS. FORT (57),
smiles ruefully.

MRS. FORT
It's better than the wicked
witch.

Cornelia opens the wardrobe, fetches the black
tailored jumpsuit she wore to the Officer's
Club the eve of the attack. She holds it up and
sadly strokes it, remembering.

CORNELIA
(to herself)
They never found Jimmy.

MRS. FORT
(oblivious)
Honey, you can't wear pants to
the Cotillion Club!

CUT TO:

INT/EXT. BLACK AND WHITE NEWSREEL MONTAGE
(REAL FOOTAGE)

Jumpy 16mm film, with a British male voice over:

Stock footage: Jackie, with glamorous models,
launches a lipstick, with exquisite art deco
wings on the packaging.

BRITISH NEWSREADER (V.O.)
American cosmetic tycooness
and world number one aviatrix
Jacqueline Cochran--

Stock footage: Jackie poses, applies lipstick
in an open cockpit plane, with "Wings to Beauty
Cosmetics" on the side.

                    BRITISH NEWSREADER (V.O.)
                Joins the war effort! Cochran
                brings American women pilots to
                White Waltham Airbase!

Jackie, in wide lapeled cream silk blouse and
pants suit, being whipped by the wind at the
air base, talks to camera.

                    JACKIE
                Today I have seen the most
                magnificent thing here in
                Britain, a very large group
                of women, the women's Air
                Transport Auxiliary--

Jackie sits on the wing of a plane, around her
in and around the cockpit, 25 attractive women
in similar attire.

                    JACKIE (V.O.)
                and I have handpicked the USA's
                top 25 aviatrixes to fly with
                them!

A very pretty American MARY NICHOLSON (33) sits
aside Jackie, green eyes and chestnut curls
styled like Jackie's.

EXT. SKY - DAY

SUPER: ABOVE SAINT-NAZAIRE PORT, OCCUPIED
FRANCE. JUNE 1942.

Above the few white clouds, a SPITFIRE - a
lithe single seater fighter plane, painted the
same azure blue as the sky.

INT. BLUE SPITFIRE - COCKPIT - CONTINUOUS

The interior looks new and unfinished. Empty
space where the radio should be. The merlin
engine PURRS happily.

Mary wears a navy ATA uniform, with flight
helmet. Her green eyes flash with concentration
underneath her goggles. She checks the ground:
a large shipping port ahead.

She checks the rear view mirror - all clear.
Checks the wings; clear. Finally she checks her
altimeter. 20,000 feet.

Mary lines her plane up carefully--

                    MARY
              (Wisconsin accent)
          4, 3, 2, 1--

As the port approaches, she presses the gun
trigger--

EXT. BLUE SPITFIRE/SKY - GUN TURRETS
- CONTINUOUS

The gun turrets are mounted with F28 cameras instead of guns. They flash with a CLICK. Then again every two seconds.

INT. BLUE SPITFIRE - COCKPIT - MOMENTS LATER

Mary finishes counting the number of photographs taken.

                    MARY
          198, 199, 200.

A sigh of relief, she checks her surrounds.
All clear. She turns over the ocean. Then pulls straight back on the stick.

EXT. SKY - DAY

The plane shoots up easily, disappearing out of sight.

INT. BLUE SPITFIRE - COCKPIT - CONTINUOUS

The altimeter reads 30,000ft. Mary pats the dashboard warmly.

                    MARY
          Good girl. Can't do that in a
          P38.

Mary checks her rear view - wait, what's that?

A khaki German Messerschmitt (ME109) bears down on her tail.

                    MARY (CONT'D)
            No no no no no no no--

She drops her speed, allows the ME109 to
catch up. She pulls her helmet and googles off
quickly, shakes her hair out.

                    MARY (CONT'D)
            Did you see me, did you see me?

Suddenly, he's aside her. She turns to the
German, gives him her brightest smile. She
takes the pins out of her hair, letting her
curls fall around her face.

                    MARY (CONT'D)
                 (behind her grin)
            Come on Fritz, let me go.

The GERMAN just stares, stunned. She braves a
wave. Waits... He breaks into a grin. Blows a
kiss. Mary blows one back. She accelerates out
over the ocean.

                    MARY (CONT'D)
            Thank Go-- (YELPS!)

The sky is grey with storm clouds ahead. She
reaches for the radio, realizes it's not there.
She swallows hard.

                                        CUT TO:

EXT. WHITE WALTHAM AIRBASE - TARMAC - DAY

SUPER: ENGLAND - WHITE WALTHAM - HEADQUARTERS
OF THE BRITISH AIR TRANSPORT AUXILIARY (ATA).
HOME OF THE ATA GIRLS.

Heavy rain and fog drown the runways.

INT. WHITE WALTHAM AIRBASE - RECREATION ROOM
- CONTINUOUS

Rain beats the windows. Pilots, male (of all
ages) and female (under 35), some in ATA
Uniform - navy pants and jacket with gold braid
- await orders. They knit, chat, or do jigsaws.

ELDERLY MAN with one arm and one eye plays
darts with a group. A MAN helps a WOMAN cut a
dress pattern on the floor.

Through an internal door enters PAULINE GOWER
(32), open pleasant face, short brown hair,
immaculate ATA uniform; with gold "SENIOR
COMMANDER" wings. Terminally jolly, posh plummy
voice, a traditional English eccentric.

Jackie, in the same uniform without the wings,
follows Pauline attentively, making notes in a
file.

                    PAULINE
          ... Can't believe the Met Office
          didn't catch the storm front.
          Over 200 *Spitfires* on the tarmac
          at Bromwich Airbase, sitting
          ducks--

                    JACKIE
        If we can't fly, the Germans
        can't--

                    PAULINE
        When it clears, would you
        like to join your girls on a
        mission?

                    JACKIE
        I would like nothing better.
        But President Roosevelt has
        requested that I observe
        operations instead.

A creak of thunder and lightening. The exterior
door is thrown open. Mary, soaking wet, leans
on a MALE ATA PILOT.

                    PAULINE
        Hallo Mary, where have you
        been?

                    MALE ATA PILOT
        She just landed a Spitfire in
        this weather! No radio. Best
        instrument flying I've ever
        seen!

                    MARY
        I *can't* fly by instruments.

He laughs. Thinks she's joking. Pauline wraps a
blanket around her.

INT. WHITE WALTHAM AIRBASE - CHANGING ROOM -
MOMENTS LATER

Pauline fetches a dry flight suit from a shelf.

                    PAULINE
          You should have jumped. You're
          much more important to us than
          any plane, even a Spit.

Mary gestures to her sopping ATA uniform. She
lifts her skirt, showing a wide gap between her
stockings and panties.

                    MARY
          I didn't want to be on display
          for all the world to see.

                    JACKIE
          Good girl.

                    PAULINE
          Stuff and nonsense!

They glance at each other. Mary disrobes.
Jackie looks away, writes notes in her book, as
Pauline rubs Mary dry.

                    JACKIE (CONT'D)
          Where's your flight suit?

                    MARY
                 (shivering)
It was urgent, Miss Cochran,
no time to change. Photo recon
over France. Need the photos
by tonight. I was the only one
available.

                  PAULINE
Get the snaps? Where's the film?

                    MARY
Just sent it with one of the
boys.

                  PAULINE
Good girl.

                   JACKIE
                 (shocked)
You flew a reconnaissance plane
into occupied territory without
express permission from your
Senior Commander?

                  PAULINE
            (before Mary can answer)
Rule 1 is we do ANYTHING we can
to serve Britain in this war.

Officially we don't do anything the actual
Air Force does - like fly recon or into enemy
territory, but rule 1 trumps all others.

                    JACKIE
          But don't you have formal
          orders?

                    PAULINE
          Yes, but we also have what we
          call the "OS," or "The Ministry
          of Odds and Sods" - which is
          any non standard request.

Jackie does a double take at Pauline's
language. She opens her mouth to speak, but
writes notes in her book instead.

                    PAULINE (CONT'D)
          We're driven by common sense,
          not bureaucracy. That's how we
          grew from 8 women to over 100.
          Avoid the military if you want
          success.

Jackie dislikes the anti-military advice. She
stops writing.

Pauline jumps suddenly. She checks her pockets,
fishes out pair of wings engraved with Jackie's
name from her pocket.

                    PAULINE (CONT'D)
          What a fool, completely forgot!
          Well done Flight Commander
          Cochran!

Seeing the shining wings, Jackie grins, all animosity over. Pauline pins the wings on Jackie's jacket with a smile.

                                        CUT TO:

EXT. EL PASO SUBURBS - DAWN

The rising sun casts a red glow onto the Franklin Mountains.

EXT. REXROAT RESIDENCE - CONTINUOUS

A modest house with dark windows. A postman stands at the door. The door opens. Rexy receives an envelope.

INT. REXROAT RESIDENCE - HALL - CONTINUOUS

Rexy walks, holding the envelope. The return address is **1st Battalion, 23rd Marines**. Rexy inhales sharply.

INT. REXROAT RESIDENCE - BEDROOM - CONTINUOUS

On the wall: DIPLOMA from the University of New Mexico, PHOTO of a girl and elderly woman in Ogala Native American dress.

A HANDSOME MAN is half-naked in Rexy's bed. She sits on the bed next to him, carefully tears open the envelope.

She reads fast. Breaks into a huge smile. As
she reads, the smile disappears. She turns over
the page.

                    HANDSOME MAN
          What's wrong?

                    REXY
          I applied to the marines. I can
          come, but they can't tell me
          what I'd be doing. Look--

She shows him the back of the letter - a list
of duties for women in the marines: cleaning,
cooking, secretarial.

                    HANDSOME MAN
          Congratulations!

Rexy tears the letter up, drops it in the
wastepaper basket.

                    REXY
          Not what I had in mind. Do you
          have any of your chocolate
          ration left?

Handsome Man finds his pants, gets a chocolate
bar. He gives it to Rexy, then takes her hand
in his. With difficulty, she unwraps and bites
the chocolate using her other hand.

                    HANDSOME MAN
          So will I see you again?

                    REXY
        Seems unlikely as you said you
        were shipping out today.

He looks sheepish. Caught in a lie. She gets
her hand free.

                HANDSOME MAN
            Well, not exactly--

She grins and takes another bite of the
chocolate bar.

                    REXY
            Have a safe trip.

                                        CUT TO:

EXT. SKY - DAY

A shiny new silver twin engine bomber (P-51
Mustang II) airplane cuts through clear blue
sky.

EXT. NEW CASTLE AIR BASE - TARMAC - CONTINUOUS

SUPER: NEW CASTLE AIR BASE, DELAWARE. UNITED
STATES ARMY AIR FORCES FERRYING COMMAND.

On the ground, awestruck pilots gaze upward in
amazement.

Betty approaches the bed, hovers without
touching it.

                    73

                    BETTY
          If my Dad catches me in here,
          he'll skin us both.

Tack nods, and caresses her hand. She holds her
breath.

                    TACK
          Gotta be back on the ARIZONA by
          first light, before I'm missed.

                    BETTY
          You can sneak in?

                    TACK
                 (laughs)
          We're not at war, it's a
          battleship, not Fort Knox.

Tack pulls her hand gently. She sinks onto the
bed. She waits, holds her breath. He kisses
her.

They drop back on the bed. She gasps as his
hand runs along her robe, he strokes her
breast, above the thin nightgown.

Betty lays back on the bed. Her eyes close...
and open again. Tack is sitting back on the
bed. He smiles.

                    TACK (CONT'D)
          I have to stop.

She looks at him quizzically, not understanding, but accepts. She stands and kisses him on the forehead.

                    BETTY
          Good night Tack.

                    TACK
          Good night Betty.

INT. JOHN ROGERS AIRPORT/PLANE - COCKPIT - NIGHT

Jimmy and Cornelia are heating up on the bench seat of the blue plane. Jimmy pulls back suddenly.

                    JIMMY
          Cornelia, I need to ask you--

                    CORNELIA
          Jimmy, Honey, please don't.

                    PILOT 1
          It's got the Alison engine
          instead of the V. So much
          power!

                    PILOT 2
          I'd give my right nut to fly
          her.

                    PILOT 1
          Yeah? I'd give something of
          value.

INT. PLANE - COCKPIT - CONTINUOUS

We see the pilot's perspective, but not their face. The interior is brand new and unfinished.

The pilot whispers a verbal checklist of actions as they prepare to land - slow and cautious. She's the exact opposite of Jackie (and also her biggest rival).

EXT. NEW CASTLE AIR BASE - TARMAC - CONTINUOUS

COL. WILLIAM H. TUNNER (36), brown hair, grey temples - makes his uniform look *good* - approaches the plane.

The pilot removes her goggles and helmet. NANCY LOVE (28), hazel eyed kewpie doll face (Clara Bow meets Marlene Dietrich), light brown hair with a silver streak, and firm handshake, which she gives to Tunner.

                    TUNNER
          How was the test, Nancy?

She hands him a neat folder of paperwork.

                    NANCY
          (Martha's Vineyard accent)
          Fabulous. Thank you, again,
          Tunner.

                    TUNNER
          Honestly, Nancy, we were hard
          pressed to find someone to fly
          her.

Nancy gestures at the men on the tarmac
watching them "what about them?" They
conspicuously look away.

                    TUNNER (CONT'D)
          Can't fly *advanced* aircraft.
          Train 'em as fast as we can,
          but we're desperate for
          experienced pilots. I'm always
          calling Hap Arnold--

Nancy stops. Tunner watches her look at all the
aircraft. She smiles. She takes Tunner's arm as
they resume walking.

                    NANCY
          Col. Tunner, I may have just
          what you need.

                                        CUT TO:

EXT. SKY ABOVE AIRPORT - EARLY MORNING

A misty morning. Two AT-6 Texans - small planes
with caged cockpits - fly dangerously close, one
above the other.

INT. AT-6 PLANE 1 - COCKPIT - CONTINUOUS

Baby faced AT PILOT 1 (17), in the lower plane, suddenly realizes he's too close. He panics and instead of pushing up on the control stick, pulls down. His plane lurches up.

                    AT PILOT 1
          ARGHHHH!

INT. AT-6 PLANE 2 - COCKPIT - CONTINUOUS

AT PILOT 2 (18) barely registers what's happening. A sickening CRASH of metal as he's hit from below. He SCREAMS.

EXT. HICKAM FIELD AIRPORT - RUNWAY - MOMENTS LATER

The two planes burn on the tarmac, mangled together. The only sound and movement, the CRUNCH of the flames.

Groundcrew fight to put out the fire. The medics wait, becoming aware they're not going to be needed.

The trainee pilots watch in horror. Betty and some typists gawk, ignoring protocol, as groundcrew try to shoo them away.

                    TYPIST
                  (to Betty)
          I can't believe you want to do
          that. Look how dangerous it is!

                    BETTY
        (tears of sadness and frustration)
         It's dangerous because they
         haven't had enough training.
         I've been trained.

INT. GENERAL HARLOW'S OFFICE - LATER

Betty stands in front of General Harlow's desk.
Harlow works on one of the piles of paperwork
in front of him.

                GENERAL HARLOW
         Yes?

                    BETTY
             (deep breath)
         Sir, I'm a trained pilot. I can
         fly anything with wings let me--

                GENERAL HARLOW
         Women can't fly in the military.
         You can't JOIN the Army Air
         Forces.

                    BETTY
         But I *type* for the military
         without joining up! Why can't I
         move planes instead? These kids
         are dying!

He looks up from his work. Assesses her. He
sighs.

                    GENERAL HARLOW
          We'd have to go through so much
          red tape, and I don't the have
          time to do it. None of us do.

                                        CUT TO:

EXT. GUILD RESIDENCE - BACK GARDEN - DUSK

Betty (still dressed in her work clothes) and
Mrs. Guild pull washing from the line.

                       BETTY
          So I quit.

Mrs. Guild keeps looking up at the sky over
Pearl Harbor.

                  BETTY (CONT'D)
          Mom, we won't be attacked
          again.

                    MRS. GUILD
          We don't know that, Bets. So,
          what will you do now? Start a
          family?

                       BETTY
          MOM, NO! I'll go with Tack to
          Philadelphia when he ships
          out, see what I can do to help
          there.

                        80

                    MRS. GUILD
          That sounds wise. Betty, choose
          your battles carefully, that's
          how to win a war. (beat) And
          also how to raise children, for
          that matter.

She winks. Betty rolls her eyes, but smiles.

                                    CUT TO:

EXT. SAVOY HOTEL - DAY

SUPER: THE SAVOY HOTEL, LONDON.

Establishing: The elegant SAVOY HOTEL on The
Strand, London.

INT. SAVOY HOTEL - JACKIE'S SUITE - DAY

Overflowing ashtrays. Thick cigarette smoke.
Empty whisky decanter. Daylight sneaks through
the curtains.

Hap Arnold sits with a US ADMIRAL (57), and
a UK AIR MARSHALL (50) wrapping a meeting.
Jackie, in her ATA uniform and wings, sits
near, not quite part of the group, not
excluded.

As the men stand to leave--

                    HAP
          Thanks for the loan of your
          room.

                    JACKIE
          My pleasure. Most of the Savoy
          is full of Ministers engaged in
          secret meetings of one nature
          or another.

The men chuckle. Jackie walks them to the door,
stares pointedly at Hap, who remains as the
other men leave.

                    JACKIE (CONT'D)
          I have done as you asked - I
          have observed the British Air
          Transport Auxiliary, commanded
          and run squadrons. I am ready
          to do the same for the USA.

She thrusts a file at Hap, shepherds him into
the corner.

                    JACKIE (CONT'D)
          You need me, Hap. We're losing
          the war, you're losing pilots.
          Fast.

Momentarily shocked, Hap concedes with a nod.

                    JACKIE (CONT'D)
          Very soon we'll need women
          pilots. Thousands of them.

                    HAP
          Thousands?

Jackie thrusts the folder open. Hap skims a list of names.

                    JACKIE
          2583 to be exact. These women
          can be military trained and
          flying for the Air Force in
          months--

Impatiently, Jackie turns the page before he can finish.

                    JACKIE (CONT'D)
          There are also 2000 more women
          with less hours. We need to
          start training IMMEDIATELY--

Jackie turns the page to designs for a military base, uniforms, a command structure. Hap steps backwards.

                    JACKIE (CONT'D)
          Ferrying, training, target
          practice, a squadron--

Hap sees the budget. Blanches at the bottom line.

                    HAP
          Jesus Jackie! There's no way in
          hell that we can afford it.

He hands the file to Jackie, makes for the door to leave.

                         JACKIE
          But Hap--

                          HAP
          The answer is NO Jackie, it's
          not going to happen.

                                        CUT TO:

INT. SAVOY HOTEL - JACKIE'S SUITE - MOMENTS
LATER

Jackie holds the telephone receiver, drums
impatiently with her manicured nails on her
desk, covered with prototypes, lipsticks,
powders, and adverts for her cosmetics range.

Suddenly, Jackie's face lights up.

                         JACKIE
          Eleanor? I need your help.

                                        CUT TO:

EXT. WASHINGTON DC - USAAF HEADQUARTERS
- DAY SUPER: UNITED STATES ARMY AIR FORCE
HEADQUARTERS.

Establishing.

INT. WASH. DC. - USAAF HQ - HAP'S OFFICE - DAY

Hap, running on very little sleep, hovers at
his huge walnut desk, a model Martin Marauder
(plane) next to him. Files everywhere. He scans

a report marked "*AIR WAR PLANS DIVISION - 42:
in order to have complete air ascendancy over
the enemy.*"

He darts to a bookcase, gets a file, compares it
to the report on the desk, sighs, puts it back,
checks another. He doesn't stop or look up. He
senses a presence in the room.

> HAP
> What's this about, Mrs. Love?

Nancy Love stands at his office door. She gently
nudges in.

> NANCY
> Welcome back, General Arnold.
> I sent you a proposal to use
> women Civilian Pilots at ferry
> command.

> HAP
> Yes, and I denied it.

> NANCY
> I wondered if you might
> reconsider.

> HAP
> Why?

                    NANCY
          They're desperate for
          EXPERIENCED pilots, and my
          girlfriends and I are sitting
          around, doing nothing.

                    HAP
          We can't afford it.

Nancy gently places a folder in front of him on
the desk.

                    NANCY
          I don't know where you got
          that idea. We'll use the same
          training structure as the men.
          The same expense as men, no
          more.

Hap slowly opens her folder, reads. It's a
simple list of women's names, a complete unit,
with a budget comparison with a male unit. The
same bottom line.

                    NANCY (CONT'D)
          We've already found
          accommodation, they have their
          own barracks.

Hap looks at her sharply.

                    NANCY (CONT'D)
        I'm afraid Tunner rather
        assumed it was a fait accompli.
        He didn't think you'd deny such
        an easy solution to an endemic
        problem.

                    HAP
        Are you aware I've denied it
        twice?

Hap regards her suspiciously. Nancy is
inscrutable.

                    HAP (CONT'D)
        Do you have enough lady pilots?
        Doesn't Jackie Cochran have the
        25 best with her in the UK?

Nancy Love stiffens at the mention of Jackie's
name.

                    NANCY
        Miss Cochran and I are very
        different pilots and we run in
        different circles. *Her* best is
        not MY best.

                    HAP
                (sighs)
        As you probably know Mrs. Love,
        the war isn't going well for
        us. We can't afford adverse
        publicity.

                              NANCY
                No risk of that. My friends
                are all nice girls, good
                backgrounds. And we can keep
                this completely quiet. Just the
                pilots you need.

Hap hesitates. Nancy sees her moment and turns
the folder to the signature page. Hap picks up
his fountain pen. It hovers

                         NANCY (CONT'D)
                At *no* additional cost.

                                              CUT TO:

INT. NAVAL BASE BEDROOM/AIR TRANSPORT FERRYING
DIVISION - DAY

A simply decorated new bedroom. Betty answers
the telephone.

                           CORNELIA
                Hey Doll. How are you?

                            BETTY
                Cornelia! Oh my, I'm so
                pleased to hear your voice.
                Philadelphia is so beautiful,
                but it's cold already--

                    CORNELIA
          Listen, never-mind
          Philadelphia. Get your ass
          down to New Castle Air Base,
          Wilmington. Nancy Love is
          getting women into the Air
          Force.

                                    CUT TO:

INT. WASH. DC. - USAAF HQ - STIMSON'S OFFICE
RECEPTION - DAY

Nancy and Tunner hover outside of the main
office door. Tunner looks at the RECEPTIONIST
(25), who is on the phone.

                   RECEPTIONIST
          Mrs. Love and Colonel Tunner
          are here, Sir... No, General
          Arnold left for the Pacific
          yesterday...

Nancy and Tunner exchange "what's going on?"
looks.

On the door a shiny brass plaque reads
"Secretary of War, HENRY L. STIMSON." The door
slowly opens.

HENRY L. STIMSON (74) tall, thin, white hair
and mustache, smart suit, exits his office,
gently closes the door.

                    STIMSON
        Hallo! Lovely to meet you both.

They shake hands. Stimson clocks how confused
they both are--

                STIMSON (CONT'D)
        I heard about your little
        experiment. Women pilots!
        Exactly what we need to
        distract the press.

                    NANCY
        The press?

PRELAP:

                STIMSON (O.S.)
        May I present, Mrs. Nancy Love,
        who will be in charge of these
        WAFS.

INT. WASH. DC. - STIMSON'S OFFICE - DAY

Stimson stands at an immense dark wood desk, a
vista of Washington DC in the windows behind
him. Nancy and Tunner stand either side, a
gaggle of reporters and photographers before
him. Stimson turns to Nancy.

                    STIMSON
        Let the gentlemen look at you.

Nancy starts, but remains composed.
Reluctantly, she walks in front of the desk,
graceful and poised. Lightbulbs go off.

                    JOURNALIST 1
          Mrs. Love, why the Air Force?

                    NANCY
          Well, flying is what I'm best
          at-- and I know a great many
          girls who, like me, love flying
          all over this country of ours
          more than anything.

She beckons to Tunner, he joins her.

                    NANCY (CONT'D)
          And there's nothing like
          knowing we're helping protect
          her.

The press LOVE her. She doesn't enjoy it, but
hides it well.

                                        CUT TO:

EXT. NEW CASTLE AIR BASE - NANCY'S OFFICE - DAY

Nancy stands in front of an office block. Behind
the block: green fields, two small planes,
personal vehicles.

An USAAF jeep pulls up. Nancy waves. Cornelia
bounces out of the jeep, carrying matched
expensive designer luggage.

                    CORNELIA
          Am I first?

                    NANCY
          Second.

                    CORNELIA
          But I jumped on the train soon
          as I got the telegram! How the
          hell--

Nancy points at a brand new pink SPARTAN
EXECUTIVE monoplane--

                    NANCY
          Barbara Du Pont flew here.

Nancy and Cornelia walk over. Heiress BARBARA
DU PONT (23), petite, beautiful black curls and
blue eyes, unloads luggage from her customized
airplane.

Barbara wears a platinum ermine fur coat.
The inside of her airplane is upholstered in
matching ermine. Barbara waves.

                    NANCY (CONT'D)
          Second is still wonderful.

EXT. NEW CASTLE AIR BASE - DAY

The USAAF jeep leaves the tarmac of the airbase
and winds along through fields past the Officers'
Club to the barracks.

INT/EXT. JEEP/NEW CASTLE AIR BASE - DAY

In the jeep, Barbara, Cornelia and HELEN
GARDNER (33) tall, elegant, strawberry blonde;
make a dignified, refined trio.

They pull up to a hastily constructed looking
two story barn built from 2 x 4s, painted pea
green.

A muddy ditch in front is covered with wooden
planks like a bridge over a moat. Cornelia puts
a saddle-shoed foot on a board. It holds. She
crosses. The others follow.

A sign reads BACHELOR OFFICERS QUARTERS (BOQ).

INT. NEW CASTLE AIR BASE - BOQ 14 - GROUND
HALL/BEDROOM- DAY

Helen opens a door. A 10x10 cubicle. A window,
no curtains. No privacy. The women exchange a
glance.

> HELEN
> We'll be entertaining the
> troops if we stay here. Let's
> try upstairs.

INT. NEW CASTLE AIR BASE - BOQ 14 - SECOND
FLOOR HALL - DAY

The women check the new rooms. Some are
brighter than others, but all are shabby,
unfinished, 10 x 10 size with sagging metal

cots, a filing cabinet and a rod to hang clothes.

Cornelia heads for the corner room.

INT. NEW CASTLE AIR BASE - BOQ 14 - CORNELIA'S ROOM - DAY

Cornelia puts her stuff on the bed to claim the room as hers.

INT. NEW CASTLE AIR BASE - BOQ 14 - SECOND FLOOR HALL - DAY

A SCREAM echoes from Cornelia's room. Helen and Barbara rush--

INT. NEW CASTLE AIR BASE - BOQ 14 - CORNELIA'S ROOM - DAY

--to find Cornelia dancing around the room.

                    CORNELIA
          Darlings! We're only IN the
          damn Air Force!

The realization hits the others. They lose their composure and join Cornelia's craziness, WHOOPING around the room.

                                        CUT TO:

INT/EXT. BLACK AND WHITE NEWSREEL MONTAGE (REAL FOOTAGE)

Footage from the Stimson meeting, Nancy, Stimson, Tunner posing happily for the camera:

                    NEWSREADER (V.O.)
          Back in the USA our girls
          aren't far behind. Nancy Love
          is the first woman in history to
          fly for the US military!

Nancy, in uniform, smiles and waves from a cockpit.

                    NEWSREADER (V.O.)
          Her WAFSs - Women's Auxiliary
          Flying Squadron - are turning
          out on the tarmac--

Cornelia, Helen and Barbara pose in front of a B-17, on the wings of planes, in the cockpit.

                    NEWSREADER (V.O.)
          They won't be spending their
          war knitting - they'll be
          delivering planes all over
          America.

INT. WEST END CINEMA - DAY

In a packed theater, Jackie watches the broadcast, mouth agape. Tears of pure rage in her eyes.

She grits her teeth. Her nails scrape into the wood chair, leaving deep scratches.

She stands suddenly, her popcorn flies everywhere. Ignoring the mess and the angry people around her, she storms out.

END OF ACT 3

ACT 4

INT. NEW CASTLE AIR BASE - DAY

Cornelia and Helen wear huge khaki zip up
overall flight suits which overwhelm even
Cornelia. A male SUPPLY OFFICER (20s) at the
counter looks at them contemptuously.

Barbara emerges from behind a door. She's
barely 5 feet. The overalls are so big the
crotch hangs down to her knees.

                    BARBARA
          Do you have anything smaller?

                    SUPPLY OFFICER
          We don't make 'em for you
          because we don't need you.

                    CORNELIA
          Charming.

Cornelia and Helen tie Barbara's belt around
her twice, bending the eyelets the wrong way
to get it to fasten. Laughing, they roll her
cuffs, but she looks like a snowman.

                    HELEN
          There must be a tailor
          somewhere.

INT. NEW CASTLE AIR BASE - GROUND SCHOOL - CLASSROOM - DAY

Cornelia, Helen and Barbara select seats among empty desks in a classroom designed for 20 students.

Ernesto - now a year older, confident in his instructor uniform - is delighted when he sees Cornelia.

> ERNESTO
>
> Cornelia!

> CORNELIA
>
> Ernesto! Don't tell me you're an instructor now.

> ERNESTO
>
> Thanks to you.

Nancy enters, hands out instruction manuals. Cornelia glances at hers; her face falls.

> CORNELIA
>
> We're not going through all this again, are we?

> NANCY
>
> Compulsory, I'm afraid.

> CORNELIA
>
> But I've *taught* this.

                         NANCY
          We're all going to have to do a
          lot of things men think we need
          to do. I think you'll find it's
          worth it.

Ernesto looks awkwardly around the room,
realization dawning.

                        ERNESTO
          Are you all qualified
          instructors?

They all nod.

                     ERNESTO (CONT'D)
          Shall we just do the test and
          go?

                         NANCY
          No chance.

Cornelia settles back into her seat and
stretches out.

                        CORNELIA
          Go on, Doll, we'll enjoy the
          show.

                                          CUT TO:

EXT. LONDON - SAVOY HOTEL - NIGHT

The elegant SAVOY HOTEL in darkness. Like the
other buildings on the street, windows are

boarded up. Street-lamps are off. Tiny FLASHES
of light in the sky.

Suddenly, a WAIL of sirens. A FLASH of light
and BOOM, then more explosions. People flee. To
the East, smoke and flames form in pockets of
the city. Jackie strides toward the hotel.

INT. SAVOY HOTEL LOBBY/RECEPTION - NIGHT

Elegant people ignore the SCREAMING air raid
sirens, and the boarded up windows. Live music
plays in the bars.

American ATA Girl Mary hovers anxiously. Jackie
strides in. Sees Mary. Slows her angry pace.
Mary rushes over to her.

                    MARY
          They've got you on a Flying
          Fortress to Montreal in 4
          hours.

                    JACKIE
          Were you able to get Hap Arnold
          on the telephone? Eleanor
          Roosevelt?

Mary shakes her head. Mary gestures to the room
around them.

                    MARY
          Telephone lines went dead.
          Should we go down to the bomb
          shelter?

                    JACKIE
        Being trapped underground
        scares me more than being blown
        up. But please, do go if you
        wish.

Jackie continues her fast pace to towards the
elevator. Mary thinks about it, then follows
her.

INT. SAVOY HOTEL - JACKIE'S SUITE - NIGHT

Jackie stuffs her suitcase angrily. Mary hovers
uselessly.

Suddenly Jackie screams, throws a file of
paperwork across the room, then sinks to the
floor, despondent.

                    JACKIE
        It's all for nothing, Mary.

Mary, terrified, has NO idea what Jackie's
talking about. She waits for Jackie to clarify,
but Jackie just sits, forlorn.

                    MARY
        What is, Miss Cochran?

                    JACKIE
        The Air Force is never going to
        approve my squadron now. That
        damn Nancy Love's SCREWED it
        all up!

Mary catches on.

                    MARY
          Oh, I'm so sorr--

                    JACKIE
          Of all the feeble minded,
          feminine, silver spoon
          bullshit. NANCY LOVE.

                    MARY
          I - er- didn't know you knew
          her.

                    JACKIE
          I don't. I know her type. We
          need a military unit. Not some
          debutante and her friends
          larking about. Oh God, they're
          training as we speak!

Mary shifts her feet uncomfortably.

               JACKIE (CONT'D)
               (looks up suddenly)
          And what will you do Mary? Will
          you go home and fly for Nancy?

                    MARY
               (surprised)
          Well, no, I haven't thought
          about it, but I don't see why I
          should.

                    JACKIE
          To fly for your country, of
          course.

Mary goes to sit on the floor next to Jackie,
then pauses. She looks to Jackie for approval.
Jackie nods.

                    MARY
          But I already fly for my
          country. Right here. We're
          fighting the same enemy as the
          Brits. What does it matter if I
          fly Spitfires in South London or
          Wildcats in Wichita?

                    JACKIE
          It's NOT the same. To wear an
          AMERICAN UNIFORM!...

                    MARY
          With all due respect, Miss
          Cochran, back home we'd be a
          million miles from the action.
          The important work is here, in
          Europe.

Jackie considers this. She sighs and starts
repacking her suitcase. Mary helps by picking
up the papers Jackie threw. Mary picks up an
advert for Jackie's cosmetics brand:

"Legstick" - leg makeup. An image of sexy
female legs, with "*Forget lipstick on his*

collar, the modern wife worries about Legstick on the back of his shirt!" written over them.

Despite herself, Mary laughs. She hands it to Jackie, who cracks a smile, just for a moment.

> JACKIE
> They must be desperate for my attention, I'd never approve that. ARGHHHH!! I've completely abandoned my cosmetics business and everything else for this.

> MARY
> Will you have time to deal with the cosmetics when you get back home?

Jackie looks sadly from the advert to her ATA wings.

> JACKIE
> I'm not ready to go back to it, but maybe I won't have a choice.

PRELAP:

> NANCY (O.S.)
> (loud but shaky voice)
> Hup, 2, 3, 4..

EXT. NEW CASTLE AIR BASE - INACTIVE RUNWAY - SUNRISE

Grey morning. The WAFS practice drills on a runway empty of planes, leading into muddy fields. Male units surround them.

Nancy looks terrified. She walks aside Cornelia, Barbara, Helen and seven other WAFS, smartly marching in grey green short gaberdine jackets, matching gored skirts and hats.

                    NANCY
              (loudest voice she can)
          Hup, 2, 3, 4...

Without moving her head Cornelia hisses to Barbara.

                    CORNELIA
          She's doing much better today.

                    BARBARA
          Poor Nancy. $5 says she messes
          up.

                    CORNELIA
          With the guys watching? No
          chance.

Nancy is starting to get the hang of it. She smiles.

                    NANCY
          Hup, 2, 3, 4, Hup, 2, 3, 4…

                    CORNELIA
          See? Oh shit.

We see Cornelia's perspective. They're
approaching the end of the runway where an
incline leads into puddles and fields.

> CORNELIA (CONT'D)
> (under her breath)
> Come on Nancy, you can do it.

Nancy beams as she watches the women marching.
She glances in front, sees the incline, gets
flustered. She looks at the male units, watching
in amusement.

> NANCY
> Uh, turn! Move! Don't...

Cornelia, Barbara and Helen are about to hit
the incline.

> CORNELIA
> It's "To the rear, March!"
> should I yell it?

> HELEN
> We've got to let her do it. How
> do you know that?

> CORNELIA
> Dad sent me to military school.
> Should we just turn?

> BARBARA
> Which way? We'll all collide!

                    CORNELIA
          You just want to win $5.

                    BARBARA
          I've already won it.

Giggling, they march down the incline into the
mud, the rest following them, in hysterics.
The male units watch in disgust. Nancy finds a
command--

                    NANCY
          HALT! SQUAD HALT!

It starts to rain.

                                        CUT TO:

EXT. NEW CASTLE AIR BASE - TARMAC - DAY

Sunny day. Cornelia, Helen and Barbara stroll
by the planes.

Male pilots sunbathe topless and drink beer- on
towels on the tarmac, on the planes. The women
stop and ogle.

                    BARBARA
          But would you look at that
          talent?

                    CORNELIA
          God bless America.

EXT. NEW CASTLE AIR BASE - TARMAC - DAY

Cornelia, Helen, Barbara and five other WAFS sunbathe in swimsuits, near the men, a little apart. Cornelia lays on the front of a fighter, Barbara next to her, both on towels.

A MALE PILOT lazing on nearby raises a beer at Cornelia, who laughs and raises a cola back.

                    MALE PILOT
          Enjoy it, could be the last
          sunny day of the year!

                    CORNELIA
          Oh we intend to!

                    BARBARA
          This is the life--

                    NANCY
          LADIES!

Nancy is flanked by three photographers and a journalist. She looks utterly displeased to be dealing with the press.

                    NANCY (CONT'D)
          These Gentlemen wish to
          photograph you. Again.

                    CORNELIA
          But it's Sunday!

The male pilots hide their beer. They're also unhappy. Some roll their eyes, some leave. The photographers start to snap.

PRELAP:

> NEWSREADER (V.O.)
> These girls have Fritz shaking
> in his boot.

INT. EL PASO CINEMA - SCREEN - NEWSREEL FOOTAGE
MONTAGE:

Shaky reportage style footage, played at
differing speeds--

A squadron of women in Russian uniforms smile
and pose.

> NEWSREADER (V.O.)
> Flying open cockpits in the
> Russian cold, without radios or
> guns, Germans call them "NIGHT
> WITCHES".

The same women decorate rickety old chipboard
and canvas airplanes - the kind not even used
as crop dusters in the USA with flowers, and
paint their lips with navigation pencils.

> NEWSREADER (V.O.)
> They only fly at night, they
> turn off their engines and
> glide so they can't be heard,
> they drop their bomb, and take
> off into darkness.

A Russian woman, bundled up warm, gets into one
to the planes, waves to camera.

                    NEWSREADER (V.O.)
          The Krauts believe Soviet
          doctors gave these women
          special powers to see in the
          dark.

Another Russian woman hands the first woman a
bomb, she casually loads it into her plane,
next to her knitting.

INT. EL PASO CINEMA - DAY

Spellbound, Rexy watches the screen. On either
side of her-- Her Ogala Native American MOTHER
(48) and SISTER (17).

Her Sister looks at Rexy's expression and then
at the screen.

                    SISTER
          Rexy, you can't even drive a
          car.

                    REXY
               (determined)
          I can learn.

Her Mother looks worriedly from Rexy, to the
screen.

                    MOTHER
          Rexy, they KILL people, do you
          understand that?

Rexy bites her lip.

                       110

EXT. PHILADELPHIA. NAVAL BASE - HOUSING
- MORNING

SUPER: PHILADELPHIA NAVEL BASE. MARRIED
OFFICERS QUARTERS.

The sun shines on a cluster of new looking pre-
fab units.

INT. PHIL. NAVAL BASE - FAMILY HOUSING -
BEDROOM - MORNING

Two cases on a double bed. Tack's military gear
is rolled and tied with string. Tack, in full
uniform, closes his case.

Betty, mature and elegant in a maroon skirt
suit and alligator pumps, closes her case. They
stare at each other.

                    TACK
          What time is—

                    BETTY
          How long till-

They laugh, releasing some tension.

Tack stands to attention and salutes Betty.
Betty returns the salute. They hold each
others' gaze.

                    BETTY (CONT'D)
          Whatever you do, do it
          carefully. I need you back.

                    TACK
          Right back at you.

Tack carries both cases out. Betty looks
around the room - their WEDDING PICTURE, soft
furnishings - their first home.

She watches Tack return. A naughty expression
in her eyes. Tack sees the expression and
raises an eyebrow.

                    TACK (CONT'D)
          Now??

                    BETTY
          Do we have time?

                    TACK
          Heck yeah!

Tack bounces onto the bed. Betty slips her
panties off and joins him. As they kiss and
fumble to get Tack's pants off:

                    TACK (CONT'D)
          I will miss you so much.

                    BETTY
          Write me whenever you can.

Betty climbs on top. Tack stops.

                    TACK (CONT'D)
         I don't even know where I'll be.

She looks at him, tears in her eyes.

                                        CUT TO:

INT. NEW CASTLE AIR BASE - OFFICERS' CLUB
- AFTERNOON

One half the room: WAFS in uniform - 20 of them
now. The rest: hostile looking women in smart
dresses. The women are all mixed together,
awkwardly, sitting at tables.

Cornelia whispers to Helen next to her.

                    CORNELIA
         What's wrong with them all?

                    HELEN
         They think we intend to steal
         their husbands.

Cornelia's eyebrows raise in surprise. She
whispers back.

                    CORNELIA
         But surely they've *seen* their
         husbands?

Helen snorts. The wives at their table look at
her sharply. At the front of the room, Nancy
stands with Col. Tunner.

                        113

                    TUNNER
          Good Afternoon Ladies! It is my
          pleasure to welcome the Women's
          Auxiliary Flying Squadron to
          the biweekly luncheon for the
          Officers' Wives. I hope this
          will be the start of a great
          friendship.

Polite applause. The wives eye the WAFSs
suspiciously.

                    TUNNER (CONT'D)
          The WAFSs are a civilian unit,
          as such, there will be no
          'mixed operation orders'--

The wives look confused--

                    TUNNER (CONT'D)
          Women will fly with women only,
          men with men--

The wives applaud loudly. Tunner can't be
heard, has to stop. Nancy is aghast at the
rudeness.

                    HELEN
                   (loudly)
          What do they think we DO in a
          cockpit? They're aware that if
          we stop flying for some nooky we
          fall out the sky?

                       114

                    CORNELIA
          To hell with this. I'm not
          going to sit here to be
          insulted.

Cornelia stands. She nods respectfully at Nancy
and Tunner, who acknowledge her ruefully. She
leaves. The WAFSs follow.

                                        CUT TO:

INT. NEW CASTLE AIR BASE - HANGAR - PT-17
COCKPIT - DAY

LT. BUDDY CHAMBERS (30), tall, blonde, ruddy,
small mustache, cheerfully nods along, as
Barbara checks instruments.

Barbara sits down into the tandem seat, plenty
of space between them. She looks expectantly at
Buddy.

                    BARBARA
          Do you think we're ready?

                    BUDDY
          Let's give it a moment.

                    BARBARA
          Sure.

Barbara scans the checklist. She notices
Buddy's thigh, which was a foot away, now
almost touches her thigh.

                      115

Alarms go off in Barbara's head. She glances
at him. He's not looking at her. She relaxes,
moves over to give him space.

Buddy looks around the hangar. No one. He turns
to Barbara, puts his hand on her leg and moves
to kiss her. Barbara backs along the seat till
she's pinned by the door.

                    BUDDY
          Don't be like that.

He kisses her. Barbara freezes, then recovers
her wits. She pushes him away; smiles politely,
not wanting to anger him.

He gently, but firmly, kisses her again, hand on
her thigh. Barbara attempts to push him away,
but can't. She goes limp.

INT. NEW CASTLE AIR BASE - BOQ 14 - BARBARA'S
ROOM - EVENING

Barbara sits on her bed, staring at a cup of
tea. Cornelia, and Helen sit next to her.

                    HELEN
          And then what happened?

INT. NEW CASTLE AIR BASE - HANGAR - PT-17
COCKPIT - DAY

Buddy tugs at the zipper on Barbara's flight
suit. He gets it to her waist, but it sticks

in her huge belt, which is still wrapped around
her twice and buckled backwards.

INT. NEW CASTLE AIR BASE - BOQ 14 - BARBARA'S
ROOM - EVENING

                    BARBARA
          He couldn't get it open and
          gave up. I froze. Saved by the
          too big flight suit and the
          fortress belt.

The rest of the WAFS have trickled into the
room, all listen intently. They don't look
shocked - just disappointed, like they knew it
was too good to be true.

                    BARBARA (CONT'D)
          He said he'd wash me out if I
          don't do it. I CAN'T get washed
          out. For the first time, I have
          a purpose.

Barbara looks at the women.

                    BARBARA (CONT'D)
          All the way back to barracks
          I kept thinking I should have
          just done it. Just this once.
          Get it over with, and then
          that's it, you know?

                    CORNELIA
          But it wouldn't be.

Helen puts her hand on Barbara's knee. Barbara
flinches, Helen puts her hand on Barbara's
shoulder, instead.

> BARBARA
>
> If I do it, I'm a whore who
> deserves what she gets. If
> don't, flying for MY COUNTRY
> isn't important enough to me...

> HELEN
>
> Reporting it's out of the
> question?

> BARBARA
>
> Nancy was clear. ANY trouble
> with the men, they'll kick *us*
> out. No gossip or scandal.

                                    CUT TO:

INT. NEW CASTLE AIR BASE - OFFICERS CLUB - LATER

The WAFS eat at one large table. They are
somber tonight.

Lt Chambers sits with two Officers and their
wives. Barbara glances over. Buddy laughs,
kisses his wife. His wife notices Barbara
looking. She glares at Barbara. Outside,
it rains.

                    END OF ACT 4

ACT 5

INT/EXT. BLACK AND WHITE NEWSREEL MONTAGE
(REAL FOOTAGE)

The Voiceover is factual, not dramatic like the
newsreels.

The word "CLASSIFIED" jumps on low quality
16mm film stock, along with the USAAF logo and
identifier numbers.

SUPER: BATAAN - PHILIPPINES - MARCH 1942

Makeshift US Army camp in recently cleared
jungle. GROUP of 20 soldiers (aged 16-25),
dirty, skinny, uniforms hanging big smile and
wave to camera. Some are injured and missing
teeth.

Same group of soldiers- fewer now, only 14 of
them- shoot at a much larger group of Japanese
soldiers.

>   VOICEOVER
>   Outnumbered, unable to reach
>   the men by air or sea, there
>   was no option but to surrender
>   these 100,000 men to the
>   Japanese.

SUPER: BATAAN DEATH MARCH - APRIL 1942

Emaciated American soldiers, tattered uniforms, march weakly, led by Japanese soldiers who look at them with disgust.

Within them: ten of the soldiers from the original group. Soldier 2 falls to the ground in a dead faint.

A JAPANESE SOLDIER bayonets him through the leg. SOLDIER 2 gains consciousness with a scream. Two of his comrades try to lift him to help him.

BANG BANG BANG - JAPANESE SOLDIER 2 shoots all three of them in the head.

SUPER: CAMP O'DONNELL - PRISONER OF WAR CAMP - MAY 1942

MASS GRAVE of Americans and Filipinos, some fresh, some skeletons. The corpse of Soldier 1 is in there. Soldier 3, skeletal and barley alive, is part of a team of prisoners, who dig the grave to make it wider.

Men with dysentery and other illnesses waste away in huts.

The footage freezes on an image of an emaciated soldier laying on the ground, looking at the camera. It's impossible to tell if he's dead or alive. The footage starts rippling...

INT. CAMP HUT - DAY

SUPER: VITI LEVU - FIJI - SEPTEMBER 1942

Small hastily constructed tent. A portable
screen and projector. Wind hits the sides of
the tent and the screen.

Hap watches from a camp bed. For the first time,
he loses his trademark smile. Hovering near
him, Army GENERAL ALEXANDER PATCH (52), tall,
grey, with a friendly bulbous nose.

> PATCH
> The Navy say they couldn't
> reach them because they don't
> have enough airplanes.

> HAP
> But why not by boat?

> PATCH
> They just say it was
> impossible.

EXT. USAAF AIRFIELD - FIJI - DAY

40 chunky camouflage painted P-39 bombers sit in
rows in cleared forest. Hap is in a jeep with
Patch. Hap is aghast.

> HAP
> If the Navy is short on planes,
> why the hell are those planes
> just sitting there? They should
> be on our aircraft carriers!

                    PATCH
              (uncomfortably)
          The Navy doesn't know what to
          do with them, Sir. Their pilots
          can't fly them.

Hap groans and pounds his fist on the dashboard.

                                        CUT TO:

EXT. NEW CASTLE AIR BASE - MORNING

Cornelia smokes surreptitiously. She's
customized her flight suit - belted it at the
waist, sewn the cuffs. She hides the cigarette
in the cuffs between puffs.

A taxi comes through security. Betty, stylish
in a maroon suit, alligator pumps and bag, gets
out. They embrace.

A group of men approach. Although one of the
men is smoking, Cornelia quickly hides her
cigarette. She hisses to Betty.

                  CORNELIA
          Ladies can't smoke on base.

Betty steps in front of Cornelia's cigarette.

                 MALE PILOT 1
               (to Cornelia)
          Hi Sugar, are you rationed?

                     122

He and his group dissolve into mocking laughter
and pass by.

                    BETTY
          That's a new one on me. What's
          it supposed to mean?

                    CORNELIA
          "Do you have a steady
          boyfriend?" It's not even the
          first time he's used it. They
          think they're funny.

Cornelia leads her towards a jeep. Betty fishes
a newspaper from her bag, opens it on the hood.
Points to a page.

THE PAGE: Full page spread of soft,
"cheesecake" style pictures of the WAFS.
Cornelia smiling from a cockpit.

                    CORNELIA (CONT'D)
          Well Damn.

There are a few pictures of Nancy, including a
low angled shot of her in a skirt, next to a
plane, focused on her legs.

The tagline reads: "NANCY LOVE, has great legs,
but is also well known for her wings."

                    BETTY
          She's up against Betty Grable
          for Best Legs 1942, apparently.

                    CORNELIA
          Do NOT mention that to her. She
          DETESTS publicly.

                                        CUT TO:

EXT/INT. NEW CASTLE AIR BASE/JEEP - DAY

Cornelia drives Betty around the Barracks -
giving a tour.

                     BETTY
          So, tell me what it's like!

                    CORNELIA
          It's been the longest week of
          my life. I-- hang on, what's he
          doing?

Another jeep approaches. Cornelia makes sure
she's far to the right so the jeep can pass.

The other jeep moves the same way, approaching
her head on. Cornelia hits the horn.

                     BETTY
          What IS he doing?

Cornelia drives closer to the right, any
further and she's in the ditch.

But the jeep coming at her does the same thing.
She steers quickly to the left, it mirrors her.

                    CORNELIA
          GET OUT OF THE WAY, JERKS!

At the last second, Cornelia steers right, into
the mud, hits a couple of bushes, with a CLUNK.
The other jeep steers left. Cornelia steers her
jeep back to the road. Turns it off.

The men, MICKEY (21) and STEVE (22), ginger but
tanned, brake, and turn to yell.

                    MICKEY
          Can't even drive a car, why do
          you think you can fly a plane?

                    CORNELIA
          Shouldn't you be fighting in the
          Pacific?

Cornelia hops out the jeep.

                CORNELIA (CONT'D)
          Or is there something wrong
          with you other than what we can
          see?

She does a quick once around the jeep. It seems
fine.

                    MICKEY
          GO HOME. We've got enough
          trouble without losing planes
          because you stuck up bitches
          want to play war!

Mickey accelerates, the jeep SQUEALS off. Betty
is hopping mad. Cornelia sighs.

                    BETTY
          HOW DO WE REPORT THEM??

                    CORNELIA
               We don't. It's their word
               against ours, they'll say we
               lost control of the jeep. Not
               worth it.

                                        CUT TO:

INT. USAAF HQ - HAP'S OFFICE - RECEPTION
- MORNING

Heather types. Hap, weather worn and weary,
strides in, begins searching files on her desk.
The phone RINGS.

                    HAP
               If it's the Navy, they can't
               have any more planes.

                    HEATHER
               Shall I tell him he's Navy, not
               Air Force, and if he wants your
               planes, he must start giving
               you his boats?

                    HAP
               I like that!

                    HEATHER
               (answering the phone)
          General Arnold's office.

                    SERGEANT (O.S.)
          This is an air-to-ground phone
          call. When you speak, I will
          flip the switch on and when
          you are finished speaking, say
          "over" and I'll flip it over.

                    HEATHER
          Yes, Sergeant. Over.

                    JACKIE (O.S.)
          Is Hap there? Over.

Heather puts her hand over the receiver.
Whispers.

                    HEATHER
          Hap, it's Jackie again.

                    HAP
               (without looking up)
            Do I look like a masochist?

Heather uncovers the phone.

                    HEATHER
          He's still in the Pacific. Over.

EXT. SKY OVER NORTH ATLANTIC OCEAN - NIGHT

A huge camouflaged B-17 "FLYING FORTRESS" four-engined plane.

INT. B-17 FLYING FORTRESS - COCKPIT - NIGHT

Jackie, in ATA uniform and Wings, speaks into the radio.

> JACKIE
> I just tried Hawaii, they said he should be back in Washington. Over.

> HEATHER (O.S.)
> He must have been delayed. Over.

Jackie hangs up the radio. Dejected.

> RADIO OPERATOR
> Say, Miss Cochran, do you still want to telephone Mrs. Roosevelt?

> JACKIE
> No, it's probably all over anyway. They won't see a reason for TWO Women's Air Squadrons.

Off her melancholy expression--

EXT. NEW CASTLE AIR BASE - TARMAC - DAY

The P-51 Mustang fighter that Nancy test flew. Far more impressive than the Oahu planes Betty

knows. Betty looks at it in wonder. Cornelia
goes to the trunk of their jeep.

                    BETTY
                  (gasps)
          But how did you get it?

                    CORNELIA
          Told them you've been grounded
          forever, so you need a
          practice flight before your test
          tomorrow.

Cornelia hands Betty a flight suit. Betty
unfolds it.

                    BETTY
          It's huge!

                    CORNELIA
          Wrap the belt around twice,
          buckle it backwards, and hope
          you don't need it.

Off Betty's quizzical look--

INT./EXT. NEW CASTLE AIR BASE - PLANE/TARMAC
- DAY

Betty helps Cornelia complete a check list.
They settle into the tandem seat.

                    CORNELIA
          Ready?

Betty nods and grins. Cornelia starts the plane, they taxi.

EXT. NEW CASTLE AIR BASE SKY/PLANE - CONTINUOUS

The P-51 leaves the tarmac, flying towards the barracks.

INT./EXT. NEW CASTLE AIR BASE SKY/PLANE
- CONTINUOUS

Cornelia hands the controls over to an ecstatic Betty.

Below them, the jerks from the jeep - Mickey and Steve - toss a football around in a muddy field near their parked jeep.

Betty squints at them. Yells to Cornelia over the engine.

                    BETTY
          Hey! Those the guys from before?

Cornelia glances down. Recognizes the jeep and men. Yells.

                    CORNELIA
          Indeed it is.

Betty aims the plane at them - descends. The plane jolts.

                    BETTY
          Wow, feel that power!

                    CORNELIA
          Betty, NO!

But Betty is determined, keeps bearing down.

                  CORNELIA (CONT'D)
          Well if I'm going down, I'm
          going down in flames.

Cornelia unzips her flightsuit. Betty grins,
gets even closer. The men scream, dive into
the mud.

Laughing, Cornelia flashes them.

Betty pulls up sharply at the last moment.

                     BETTY
          Sometimes you've got to put
          them in their place.

                    CORNELIA
          Honey, sometimes you've got to
          rise above it. Are you trying
          to get washed out before you
          even start?

Betty hadn't thought of this. Worry crosses her
face. Oblivious, Cornelia laughs and zips up.

                                        CUT TO:

EXT. NEW CASTLE AIR BASE - TARMAC - LATER

                      131

Grey day. In the cockpit of her silver AT-6 fighter with a khaki nose, Barbara does final checks, nails oil-stained.

Around her, male and female pilots and ground crew work the busy runway. Buddy watches Barbara as she jumps down from her cockpit, and walks over to talk to Ernesto.

                                        CUT TO:

EXT. AIR FORCE BASE - WASHINGTON DC - TARMAC - DAY

MAVIS JACKSON (20), pretty former farm girl, now an Air Force secretary. She wears a neat uniform, but her auburn hair isn't set right, and her make up skills are lacking.

Mavis chews on a pen as she watches airmen exiting a camouflaged B-17 "FLYING FORTRESS".

Jackie exits - looking tired and worried - and heads straight for a waiting car, parked on the tarmac.

Mavis makes a beeline for Jackie, thrusts a picture at her.

                    MAVIS
            (rural Wisconsin accent)
        Miss Cochran, I am so sorry to
        disturb you, but could I please
        have your autograph?

                      132

Jackie looks at her in surprise.

> JACKIE
> Well sure.

Jackie signs the picture. She sizes Mavis up,
clocking her working class background and her
make up flaws. She reaches into her bag and
brings out a tissue. Holds it up to Mavis.

> JACKIE (CONT'D)
> May I?

Bewildered, Mavis nods. Jackie takes the tissue
and blends the foundation on Mavis's jawline.
It's too dark.

> JACKIE (CONT'D)
> This is the wrong color for
> you. And it's a cheap pigment.
> Here--

Jackie opens her case and brings out a new,
lighter foundation. Smoothes it on Mavis's
face.

> JACKIE (CONT'D)
> So if you're not a fan of my
> *cosmetics*, are you a fan of
> flying?

> MAVIS
> I love flying more than
> anything.

Jackie holds the mirror for Mavis to admire
Jackie's work.

                    JACKIE
          Really? You fly?

                    MAVIS
          Been flying crop dusters since
          I was 13.

Jackie raises an eyebrow. She hands Mavis the
foundation, and as an afterthought, gives her
some better lipsticks, too.

                    JACKIE
          Keep them. So why haven't you
          joined Nancy Love's flying
          squad?

                    MAVIS
            (completely flustered)
          Oh thank you Miss Cochran! I
          can't join - that is, you have
          to be invited - and you have to
          be friends with Nancy, or know
          someone who is. It isn't for
          girls like me.

Jackie snorts. Thinks about it. Breaks into a
slow determined smile. She's found her purpose
again.

                    JACKIE
          Oh isn't it? Miss, could you
          get me Eleanor Roosevelt on the
          telephone?

Off Mavis' surprise--

EXT. NEW CASTLE AIR BASE - TARMAC - DAY

The tarmac is full of planes waiting fly.
Cornelia waits in her cockpit. Ahead of her,
Barbara takes off.

INT./EXT. PLANE COCKPIT/NEW CASTLE AIR BASE SKY
- CONTINUOUS

Barbara reaches altitude, she reaches with her
left hand to adjust the throttle. The whole
panel comes off in her hand.

Horrified, she stares at the panel. It's still
hooked up to the throttle and prop. If she lets
go it will dislodge them.

In her right hand, she holds the control stick.
She can't let go of that, either.

The plane staggers a bit - she HAS to get
the flaps up, but she can't. She looks at her
control panel, then her radio.

Barbara pushes the control stick, the plane
climbs, stuttering, and she levels it off.

She wraps her thighs around the control stick, holding it with all her force. With her right hand she hits the radio.

>   BARBARA
>   This is 106. My control panel
>   is broken and I need to land.
>   Over.

>   TOWER
>   We're clearing you. Where will
>   you go down? Over.

INT./EXT. PLANE COCKPIT/NEW CASTLE AIR BASE SKY
- CONTINUOUS

>   BARBARA
>   Can't use the throttle, prop
>   or mixture. Will come down
>   at speed and try to stick the
>   landing. Over.

Barbara switches off the radio, careful not to move the panel in her left hand. She takes the control stick, in her right, lets go with her thighs. She eases into descent with it.

Loose screws from the panel CLANK as they roll on the floor.

EXT. NEW CASTLE AIR BASE - TARMAC - CONTINUOUS

Cornelia joins a group including Ernesto, Mickey and Steve, who look scared, eyes glued to Barbara in the sky.

                    MICKEY
          Women just shouldn't FLY. They
          put everyone in danger.

She splutters through a wide circle, heads
toward the runway.

INT./EXT. PLANE COCKPIT/NEW CASTLE AIR BASE SKY
- CONTINUOUS

Without realizing, Barbara mutters to herself
as she pushes the AT-6 down, focusing on
keeping the tachometer level.

                    BARBARA
          Come on come on come on come
          on...

Below her she sees the barracks, then fields.
She approaches the runway at a good angle; but
much too fast.

The plane lurches down, Barbara nearly loses
her lunch, but she swallows, holds the control
stick so tightly blood comes out from under her
stark white knuckles.

Barbara blacks out. DARKNESS. SILENCE. A beat.

The world returns, the plane SHRIEKING louder,
the ground much closer. She clears trees, then
a fence.

She braces herself, pulls back on the control stick with all her being, gets the plane as flat to the runway as possible.

EXT. NEW CASTLE AIR BASE - TARMAC - CONTINUOUS

Everyone holds their breath.

INT./EXT. PLANE COCKPIT/NEW CASTLE AIR BASE - CONTINUOUS

THWACK. The plane hits the tarmac. Bounces. Lands flat again.

Stationary planes create an impossibly tight corridor. As Barbara speeds through them they SHUDDER and RATTLE.

EXT. NEW CASTLE AIR BASE - TARMAC - CONTINUOUS

A cheer rings out in the crowd.

INT./EXT. PLANE COCKPIT/TARMAC/FIELD - CONTINUOUS

Barbara holds tight. The runway is too short, the plane runs off the tarmac and into the fields.

Barbara slams through a barbed wire fence, comes to a stop.

She sits frozen, still gripping the control panel in her left hand and the control stick in her right.

Suddenly - a crowd outside the plane. Medics
try to free her. MEDIC pries Barbara's hand
from the panel, Ernesto takes the panel from
her. Cornelia and Helen help Barbara out.

Medic checks Barbara over quickly. Mickey looks
at the control panel in amazement.

>   MICKEY
>   How the hell did you land
>   it????

>   MEDIC
>   She's fine!

A CHEER from the crowd, everyone looks at
Barbara with respect. Ernesto and Mickey
examine the control panel.

>   MICKEY
>   I flew her this morning. The
>   panel was NOT loose then.

A hush goes through the crowd. A LT. SERGEANT
pushes through.

>   LT. SERGEANT
>   Clear the area!

Mickey hands a screw from the plane to LT.
SERGEANT.

                    MICKEY
          These are all through the
          cockpit. What are the odds of
          them all coming loose at once?

                    BARBARA
          I did a flight check beforehand.
          Twice in fact. Everything was
          great. Then I left to get my
          scarf--

                    CORNELIA
          Oh come on, can there really
          be anyone here who finds MURDER
          less offensive than a woman
          pilot?

Her face changes as she realizes that's EXACTLY
the situation. The men look as horrified as the
women. Everyone looks around at each other. Who
could it be?

                    LT. SERGEANT
          Clear the area immediately!

Slowly, the crowd disperses. Mickey sides up to
Cornelia.

                    MICKEY
          I'm so very sorry. I was just
          messing around this morning. I
          wasn't trying to hurt anyone.

                        140

Cornelia looks at him. He's more shocked than she is. She wants to tell him off, but suddenly she's very tired.

                    CORNELIA
          I know.

                    MICKEY
          She's one hell of a pilot.

                    CORNELIA
                  (tired smile)
          I know.

Buddy watches Barbara with a cold look on his face. He doesn't notice Cornelia is watching him.

                                        CUT TO:

INT. NEW CASTLE AIR BASE - NANCYS OFFICE - DAY

Betty, back in her suit and pumps, hair a little messier, nervously sits opposite Nancy.

                    NANCY
          I hear you fancy yourself as
          something of a stunt pilot.

Betty is shocked. Did Nancy see her?

                    NANCY (CONT'D)
This is a military base,
Mrs. Tackaberry. Word gets
around. My WAFSs must be above
reproach. I've been working on
this for too long to risk it
for anything.

                    BETTY
Yes Ma'am.

                    NANCY
Buzzing anyone will get you
automatically washed out.

Betty swallows, scared Nancy will dismiss her.
Nancy takes pity on her, gives her a slow
smile.

                    NANCY (CONT'D)
Well, we can't wash you out
before you begin. But you
must grow up- you only get one
chance here. The men can be a
little... tricky. Can you let
it all roll off you like water
off a duck's back?

Betty smiles and nods.

                    NANCY (CONT'D)
Wonderful. Now, your paperwork?

Betty is overjoyed. She hands Nancy her
paperwork.

                    NANCY (CONT'D)
            Letters of reference...

She scans them quickly.

                    NANCY (CONT'D)
            College education, and you're
            21?

Betty nods, getting more excited.

                    NANCY (CONT'D)
            Commercial license, 200
            horsepower rating...

Nancy flicks through the logbook. She stops,
alarmed.

                    NANCY (CONT'D)
            You have 450 hours?

                    BETTY
            Y-yes. I need 300 hours, don't I?

                    NANCY
            I'm so sorry, no you need 500.

                    BETTY
            But I read the application--

                    NANCY
          My Dear, that was written for
          men. Men need 200, women need
          500.

                                        CUT TO:

INT. NEW CASTLE AIR BASE - HALL - DAY

Betty walks out of Nancy's office, shaking,
but trying to hold it together. She looks for
the bathroom. She finds it, checks no one's
watching, and ducks inside.

INT. NEW CASTLE AIR BASE - BATHROOM - DAY

As Betty enters the toilets, her tears start
flowing. She notices smoke coming from a stall.
She pauses, puzzled.

Betty looks under the door and sees a pair of
saddle shoes with the rolled cuffs of a flight
suit.

                    BETTY
          Cornelia?

Cornelia opens the door, regards Betty's tears
with shock.

                   CORNELIA
          Bets?

                    BETTY
          I don't have enough hours.

                    144

Cornelia hands Betty her cigarette. Betty looks at it for a moment, then takes a drag. Cornelia uses the cuffs of her flight suit to wipe Betty's tears. She looks her in the eyes.

                    CORNELIA
          You will.

Betty smiles slowly.

                                        CUT TO:

INT./EXT. WASH. DC. - USAAF HQ - ENTRANCE - DAY

Jackie marches towards two sentries guarding the entrance. They stand to attention for her. She passes, waving a UK ID.

                    SENTRY 1
          Do we stop her?

                    SENTRY 2
                (shrugs)
          That's Jackie Cochran, I'm not
          stopping her.

INT. WASH. DC. - USAAF HQ - RECEPTION - DAY

Jackie marches past reception and into the elevator.

INT. WASH. DC. - USAAF HQ - HAPS OFFICE RECEPTION - DAY

JACKIE throws opens the door, marches past
Heather--

> HEATHER
> He's on the telephone Miss
> Cochran!

> JACKIE
> Really? I didn't think he
> answered the telephone!

Off Heather's embarrassment--

INT. WASH. DC. - USAAF HQ - HAPS OFFICE - DAY

Jackie barges in. Seeing Hap IS on the phone,
she hovers.

> HAP
> Mr. President, I know the
> Japanese attacked Australia,
> but--

Hap listens. Jackie tries to eavesdrop.

> HAP (CONT'D)
> We can redirect the planes, but
> we don't have the manpower--

At "manpower," Jackie looks pointedly at Hap.
He sighs.

Yes, Sir. That is a wonderful
suggestion. But what about
the funding it? Oh really?
(Hap smiles) Please thank the
First Lady for her assistance.
(Pauses) Thank you, sir. I'll
get right on it.

As he hangs up, Jackie launches at him.

JACKIE
You let Nancy set up this
ridiculous sorority unit?

HAP
I--

JACKIE
I know you think this is a
vanity project for me, but it's
about saving lives. Think of
all the men who died in the
Philippines because we couldn't
fly supplies to them.

HAP
Jack--

                    JACKIE
          The ONLY way to get the
          manpower to hold the Pacific AND
          defeat Germany is with a force
          of women delivering airplanes
          from the factories, ferrying,
          teaching, and leading target
          practice so that every single
          able bodied man we have is at
          the front, fighting the enemy!

                    HAP
          Jackie, will you let me--

                    JACKIE
          Nancy's little group of
          ferrying friends is a nice
          start, but *woefully* inadequate.
          We need a real leader, and
          women pilots taking over
          EVERYTHING but combat. You need
          me Hap!

                    HAP
          JACKIE!

He gives his winning smile. His eyes sparkle
despite fatigue.

                    HAP (CONT'D)
          You win.

Jackie covers her mouth with her hand, dazed.

                    JACKIE
          I win what?

                    HAP
          The President will fund your
          plan. You'll work directly out
          of my office. Let's train 5000
          women!

Jackie manages a weak smile, but then her eyes
narrow.

                    JACKIE
          Hap, this time I want it in
          writing so you can't weasel out
          of it.

Hap picks up the phone.

                    HAP
          Heather? Need to dictate a
          memo. Also, have Tunner, George
          and Smith report to my office
          ASAP. And ring Sweetwater,
          tell them we're setting up base
          there.

Jackie grins as she collapses into the chair
opposite him.

                    JACKIE
          Where the hell is Sweetwater?

INT. INDIO, CA - COCHRAN/ODLOM RANCH - DRAWING
ROOM - DAY

The "House that Jackie Built" - split level, colored stone, expensive rugs, a rare combination of beauty and comfort - it's a gorgeous *home*, not just a gorgeous house.

Seated reading: CEO of RKO Pictures, 5ft 8 FLOYD ODLUM (60, but looks 50), balding grey hair, pleasant round face, glasses, in a white bathrobe covered in orange palm trees.

A car PULLS UP. Floyd drops his book. With a little effort, he gets himself onto his feet as Jackie enters.

                    FLOYD
          Darling! This is a surprise.

They embrace, passionately. Jackie relaxes into him.

                    JACKIE
          Didn't you get my cable?

                    FLOYD
          The one that just read
          "Darling. Coming Home"?

Jackie giggles. It's the first time we've heard her giggle.

                    JACKIE
          What kind of wife would I be if
          didn't keep you in suspense?

He smiles, utterly besotted. She returns his look.

                    FLOYD
          I've had cocktails set up by
          the big pool. Unwind and tell
          me all.

They walk, arm in arm, Jackie stops. She looks the mantelpiece. A doll stands in a glass case. Floyd lets Jackie go. She walks over to it, and touches the glass.

In contrast to everything else in the house, the doll is *old*; restored porcelain with blonde curls, brown eyes, pearly skin, and a new outfit. Jackie smiles at her lovingly.

                              FLASH CUT:

CLOSE ON: Jackie, as a six year old, holds the doll in her hands. Jackie's fingers are wrapped with bloodied bandages.

PRELAP: slow jazz cover of Kate Bush's THIS WOMANS WORK.

EXT. SWEETWATER, TEXAS - AVENGER FIELD MILITARY BASE - DAY

A hastily constructed military base stands silently on orange desert dirt. A Texan rattlesnake slithers along.

The stillness is disturbed as one, then two
cattle trucks pull into the base, stirring up
clouds of dust.

Mavis, in her best suit, her make up vastly
improved, carries a suitcase. She is the first
to jumps down from the truck.

She looks up in awe. She strides proudly
towards the arches of the main building. 50
women with suitcases follow her.

In the second cattle truck, Betty, with her
alligator bag, jumps to the ground. 50 women
with suitcases follow them.

Reveal in slow motion: in big letters on the
arches of the main building, the words "AVENGER
FIELD". The women go under the arches, proudly
answering their call to war.

END OF PILOT

What follows is a report from top script assessment service WeScreenplay on Avenger Field Pilot Episode.

—WESCREENPLAY

Entry Type: Basic Coverage (WeScreenplay)
Synopsis Included: No
Notes Date: June 28th, 2020
Analyst: SMA1
Ranking: 99th Percentile

AVENGER FIELD

Drama | Television (One-hour) | 87 Pages

Written by: Kimberley Kates & Catherine Taylor

Created by:
Kimberley Kates, Sandro Monetti,
Catherine Taylor

TOP 1%
CONCEPT

TOP 1%
DIALOGUE

TOP 1%
CHARACTERS

RATING
RECOMMEND
PLACED IN THE TOP 1%

Percentiles are based on historical data of scores given out by this analyst.

For increased consistency, we calculate a project's pass/consider/recommend rating by using the scores input by the analyst and their history of scoring. Approximately 3% of projects receive a recommend and ~20% of projects receive a consider.

WeScreenplay proudly uses Coverfly, an online platform that connects writers, readers, and the industry.

OPENING THOUGHTS

This pilot is a unique and original dramatization of the advent of women pilots in World War II, which comes off as both meticulously researched and ripe in its potential to launch a captivating, tense, and powerful series.

CHARACTERS

The pilot showcases a broad cast of characters, most if not all of whom are based on real individuals who served in World War II. Apart from coming off as inspiring and relatable leads, Cornelia, Betty, Jackie and Nancy are all strongly developed: each of these four main characters receive a well-balanced amount of page time in relation to one another, and it felt easy to keep track of their storylines (and their interconnectivity) despite the script's frequent time-jumps and changes of locale. Barbara stands out as a strong supporting character, and Helen and Mavis are well-established as interesting characters who will likely get their chance to shine in future episodes. One character that could use some more work is Rexy. Her first scene at the close of Act II is great: Mae's accident is jarring and a good point of action in the script, and Rexy's reaction to it proves to be a strong introduction to her character. However, she disappears for a while after this and doesn't show up again until a scene where we see her family disapprove of her military aspirations; after this, Rexy doesn't show up again in the pilot. While the real life Ola Rexroat is most assuredly an important character to be included in this story, Rexy feels somewhat underdeveloped in this pilot and her story in the episode doesn't really have a button on it: one possible solution would be if we saw her in the end scene with Mavis in the new recruits. Better yet, though, and to address the writer's concern about the length of the pilot, Rexy could be removed from the pilot and more thoroughly introduced in episode two or further episodes. While it may be painful to consider removing Rexy from the pilot, at the same time it would ease some of the weight of all the other characters' storylines and open up space for further development of the main dramas at play.

PLOT

The plot of this pilot is very solid, which is no easy feat for such a complex story. Act I is teeming with tension, which erupts as the attack on Pearl Harbor unfolds before Cornelia and Betty's eyes at the climax of the act. This sets the tone for the script going forward, as the trauma of war is juxtaposed with the challenge that the women face in trying to break the glass ceiling in the military. As the story unfolds, the use of newsreels and archival footage is perfect in creating an immersive period piece, and reinforces the thrill of watching a story that has yet to be told in mainstream television. The five act structure is put to great use, with each act closing on a dramatic and memorable high note. While the script hits most of the right beats, the scenes tend to be pretty short, and there are a few moments where a transition to a new scene feels rushed, or like the current scene needs to breathe a bit more before going to a new one. One such example is when Cornelia rings Betty to tell her that Nancy is getting women into the Air Force. At this point we haven't seen Cornelia in almost 20 pages, having last seen her in a newsreel -- thus her sudden appearance to call Betty feels under-informed as we haven't caught up with Cornelia, and the conversation seems cut short when it may have been an opportunity to explore the emotions they feel at finally getting their chance to prove themselves as pilots. Another note regarding the plot is that there are three separate instances showcasing harrowing plane landings: first Cornelia, then Jackie, then Barbara. Naturally, a show about aviators is expected to have a healthy amount of such white-knuckle situations involving the landing of a plane against all odds, but it may be worth it to find a way to further distinguish those scenes from one another, lest these action points come off as same-y or repetitive. Finally, Betty's storyline in the pilot could use a better button: she is told near the end that she doesn't have enough practice hours to fly, but that conversation is abruptly cut short and we then see Betty in the final scene leading the new recruits to the base without her lack of hours being further addressed. This is a minor detail, but her arc in the pilot would feel more complete if she acknowledged the fact that she has more work to do, perhaps in the context of a conversation with Cornelia or Nancy.

DIALOGUE

The dialogue is spot-on throughout this pilot. The emotions and intentions of each main character are crystal clear and the dialogue feels naturalistic, practical, and never forced. There is potent subtext to the characters' lines, with dialogue coming off as deliberate and restrained rather than overt or on the nose. One thing that could use some more development in the second half is the relationship between Cornelia and Betty, which receives a good deal of attention in the first few acts but peters out a bit toward the end, where they don't have as many scenes together. A sisterhood is established between them early in the script that can be capitalized on in the final two acts, once they're in the thick of their military operations. The derogatory and discouraging actions of the men around them in the final two acts present a good opportunity for Cornelia and Betty to reflect together. The attack on the Jeep, the rude comments from the man giving them their suits, catcalls from enlisted men and Barbara's assault at the hands of Buddy are all topics that the two of them may wish to unpack with each other, providing a moment of catharsis in the script and reaffirming the importance of the women's drive and perseverance in a way that represents the central message of the story. Jackie has a great moment like this during her interaction with Mavis, where Jackie realizes that women like Mavis are the reason she fights -- this serves the function of reaffirming the story's message, but Cornelia and Betty (as the first characters we meet) feel deserving of a moment like this too, perhaps after Barbara tells her Buddy story or after Barbara's plane is sabotaged. Ultimately, while Cornelia, Betty, Jackie and Nancy are all very strong leads, Cornelia and Betty feel more like the protagonists of the story, which is why a reflective conversation between the two of them later in the pilot could prove to be engaging and emotional, further investing us in these characters.

CONCEPT

The concept of Avenger Field is not only unique and marketable, it is a story that needs to be told. Despite the fact that war dramas (especially

156

those relating to World War II) are a dime a dozen in Hollywood, this story is exceptionally important in that it tells the story of a real group of women who left a lasting impact -- not only on women's role in the US military, but on the right of women to thrive in fields that were historically dominated by men. The pilot sets the stage for a captivating series that will be powerful, uplifting, and probably heartbreaking as the real life Cornelia Fort died in 1943, just six months after the events of this pilot, and two years before the conclusion of World War II. It is interesting to think about how this will be addressed in the series -- will it conclude with Cornelia's death, will it highlight the continuing story of the rest of the team as they pick up the pieces after the loss of their friend, or will it venture into a totally new territory, an alternate history where Cornelia ended up surviving the incident that took her life The concept of Avenger Field shines as a true story that is underreported, which itself feels like something that needs to be corrected. While it may not feel like the most "urgent" story in need of telling during our current time, there's something to be said about the fact that many of these women, some of whom only passed away as recently as the 2010's, have not had their moment to shine in the way that other World War II heroes (both male and female) have had.

FINAL THOUGHTS

All in all, Avenger Field is a gripping and high-quality pilot, which has all the hallmarks of a series that will not only sell, but has the potential to inspire a new generation of women.

STRUCTURE

Structurally, the pilot is near to perfection, which again is no easy feat given the challenge of telling a story across multiple countries with a subject as massive as World War II and the moving pieces that come with it. The main kinks in the structure were alluded to in the "Plot" and "Characters" sections: the need to constantly change location can sometimes encroach on dialogue, with some potentially remarkable conversations being cut short, resulting in the feeling that the story is moving a hair too fast. Additionally, as stated before, the underdeveloped presence of Rexy adds another layer to the pilot that doesn't quite pay off at the end, and her story is probably best introduced and expounded upon in the second episode, which can free up page space to let some of the other drama breathe a bit more.

AVENGER FIELD

VIRTUALLY PERFECT	EXCELLENT	GOOD	IMPROVE
98th - 100th Percentile	85th - 97th Percentile	50th - 84th Percentile	0th - 49th Percentile
Plot 99th Percentile	**Structure** 96th Percentile	-	-
Concept 100th Percentile			
Dialogue 99th Percentile			
Characters 99th Percentile			

RATING

RECOMMEND

PLACED IN THE TOP 1%

ABOUT STORY ANALYST SMA1

Former reader at HBO and Pipeline Entertainment. Currently writing, directing, and film editing.

Percentiles are based on historical data of scores given out by this analyst.

For increased consistency, we calculate a project's pass/consider/recommend rating by using the scores input by the analyst and their history of scoring. Approximately 3% of projects receive a recommend and ~20% of projects receive a consider.

WeScreenplay proudly uses Coverfly, an online platform that connects writers, readers, and the industry.